M000105981

Charles A. Hewlett and Gadi Kaufmann

Foreword by Christopher Leinberger

Strategy for Real Estate Companies

ULI–the Urban Land Institute
1025 Thomas Jefferson Street, N.W.
Suite 500 West
Washington, D.C. 20007-5201

Library of Congress Cataloging-in-Publication Data

Hewlett, Charles A.
Strategy for real estate companies / Charles A. Hewlett and Gadi Kaufmann ; foreword by Christopher B. Leinberger.
p. cm.
ISBN 978-0-87420-997-6 (alk. paper)
1. Real estate business—Management. 2. Strategic planning.
I. Kaufmann, Gadi. II. Title.
HD1375.H53 2008
333.33068'4–dc22

2008003467

10 9 8 7 6 5 4 3 2 1

Printed in the United States of America

About ULI—the Urban Land Institute

The mission of the Urban Land Institute is to provide leadership in the responsible use of land and in creating and sustaining thriving communities worldwide. ULI is committed to

- Bringing together leaders from across the fields of real estate and land use policy to exchange best practices and serve community needs;
- Fostering collaboration within and beyond ULI's membership through mentoring, dialogue, and problem solving;
- Exploring issues of urbanization, conservation, re-generation, land use, capital formation, and sustainable development;
- Advancing land use policies and design practices that respect the uniqueness of both built and natural environments;
- Sharing knowledge through education, applied research, publishing, and electronic media; and
- Sustaining a diverse global network of local practice and advisory efforts that address current and future challenges.

Established in 1936, the Institute today has more than 40,000 members worldwide, representing the entire spectrum of the land use and development disciplines. ULI relies heavily on the experience of its members. It is through member involvement and information resources that ULI has been able to set standards of excellence in development practice. The Institute has long been recognized as one of the world's most respected and widely quoted sources of objective information on urban planning, growth, and development.

ULI Project Staff

Rachelle L. Levitt
Executive Vice President, Global Information Group
Publisher

Dean Schwanke
Senior Vice President
Publications and Awards

Nancy H. Stewart
Director, Book Program

Lori Hatcher
Director, Publications Marketing

Lise Lingo
Publications Professionals LLC
Manuscript Editor

Betsy VanBuskirk
Art Director

Anne Morgan
Graphic Design

Craig Chapman
Director, Publishing Operations

The Authors

Charles A. Hewlett is managing director of RCLCO (Robert Charles Lesser & Co., LLC). He has more than 25 years of experience in real estate and has consulted on a broad spectrum of commercial and residential properties in most major metropolitan regions of the United States. Before joining RCLCO, he was president of Lofty Builders, Inc., a real estate service company concentrating in renovation, rehabilitation, and management of investment real estate properties in the Boston metropolitan area. Hewlett leads RCLCO's strategic planning practice. He has conducted training seminars on the methodology for conducting metropolitan-development trend analysis for regional branch offices of major national commercial developers. He also is a frequent speaker, has served on a number of ULI Advisory Services panels, and has written articles published in the *Corridor Real Estate Journal*, *Urban Land Digest*, and publications of the National Multi Housing Council (NMHC). Hewlett is an advisory member of the NMHC and a full member of ULI. He is a graduate of Brown University. RCLCO is a ULI sustaining member firm.

Gadi Kaufmann is the chief executive officer of RCLCO. He has been a guiding force behind the firm's expansion into an end-to-end solutions provider to the real estate industry and a leader in advancing performance strategy for real estate companies, portfolios, and projects around the world. Since joining the firm in 1979, Kaufmann has managed thousands of engagements for privately held and publicly traded companies, and for public sector and government entities. He specializes in economic consulting for real estate projects and portfolios; corporate strategy planning and management consulting; transactional and negotiation services; and financing and capital formation and implementation. Kaufmann is a trustee of the Urban Land Institute and a governor of the ULI Foundation. He has been an active member of the Young Presidents' Organization (YPO), serving in various leadership positions in YPO chapters in southern California and the Washington, D.C., region, and on YPO's International Board of Directors and its Northeastern U.S. Regional Board. He also serves on the International Board of Chief Executives Organization. In 2006, Kaufmann became a founding member of the board of the Richard S. Ziman Center for Real Estate at the University of California–Los Angeles, from which he earned a B.A. in economics.

Acknowledgments

Gadi and I would like to first thank our friend and colleague Chris Leinberger who, to the best of our knowledge, invented strategic planning specifically for real estate companies back in the early 1980s. We both learned the practice from Chris, and Gadi and I have tried to continue his legacy by attempting to take strategy planning for real estate companies to the next level with every new opportunity.

This book is also the result of strategic planning and implementation consulting that our firm, RCLCO (Robert Charles Lesser & Co.), has conducted over the past three decades. The firm conducts more than 500 engagements per year in nearly every major metropolitan region in the United States and abroad, spanning every real estate product type and company size, ownership type, etc. This asset-level consulting work has provided tremendous insights into the types of issues that real estate companies face and the strategic-level thinking that occurs in some of the most influential companies in the industry. With this in mind, we would also like to thank our many clients for the opportunity to work closely with them on both asset-level and company-wide strategic consulting engagements over the years. The list is too long to include in its entirety here, but we would especially like to thank Bryce Blair of AvalonBay, Tom Bozzuto of the Bozzuto Group, Todd Mansfield of the Crosland Group, and Robert Duncan of Transwestern, all strategy clients of RCLCO who agreed to have their company strategy experiences told in the form of case studies in the appendix and elsewhere in the book.

We would also like to thank our Board of Advisers, who were invited to comment on and critique this book, which they did with insight, candor, and considerable effort. These reviewers included Ron Terwilliger of Trammell Crow Residential; Stephen Blank, senior fellow of the Urban Land Institute; Lizanne Galbreath of Starwood; and Harry Frampton of East West Partners. The comments we received were very much appreciated and taken into consideration during the editing process.

A number of our RCLCO colleagues provided input and assistance for the book, for which we are extremely grateful. They include Laura Cole, who helped keep us on track; Bethany Perry, who kept us organized; Michelle Loutoo, who tracked down obscure data; Elizabeth Davidson, who served as a valued internal sounding board; and Gregg Logan, Bob Gardner, and Melina Duggal, who helped us reach out to clients for interesting case study stories that help bring the book to life.

Finally, but by no means last in order of importance, I would like to thank Julie Stern, who was instrumental in making this book happen. She provided editing input and guidance, creativity, and perseverance throughout the six-month process of producing this work. Simply put, without Julie's help, this book would not have been possible. Thank you.

Charles A. Hewlett
Managing Director
RCLCO

Contents

Contents

Foreword

The original version of this book was conceived and written in the early 1990s. In retrospect, that time period saw the most important transition for the real estate industry since the 1930s. Few of the changes that took place then were reflected in the original book, since no one knew what the consequences of those changes would be for the strategic plans of companies in the industry. We were busy making it up as we went along—and trying to survive. Hence, a revision of this book on strategic planning for real estate companies is overdue as a result of these changes alone.

It is important to reflect on the changes that took place in the real estate industry during the early 1990s, both to understand them and to put into context a less wrenching but no less significant change that is occurring as this version of this book goes to press in 2007. The 1980s saw the largest real estate boom in American history. When it came to an end, the worst real estate downturn since the Great Depression of the 1930s ensued. Virtually every product type in real estate—office, industrial, retail, for-sale housing, rental housing, hotels—saw market demand collapse in the early 1990s, leading to skyrocketing vacancy rates and plummeting rental rates and sales prices. Vacancy rates for office space rose well above 20 percent in most markets and sometimes above 40 percent. Sale prices in many formerly hot housing markets such as California and the

Northeast declined in the 1990s for the first time since the 1930s. On average, properties lost approximately 30 percent of their value; some suffered losses of 50 percent or more. According to standard economics, when the level of economic activity drops by more than 20 percent, the economy is officially in a depression. The early 1990s were a real estate depression.

The 1980s boom had been financed by banks, insurance companies, and international investors, but most infamously by savings and loans. As a retrospective Federal Deposit Insurance Corporation study stated, this crisis was "the greatest collapse of U.S. financial institutions since the 1930s." The early 1990s financial crisis—which affected not only the real estate industry but also the budget stability of the federal government and the overall economic performance of the nation—was the defining moment of the past half-century for the U.S. real estate industry. This near financial meltdown marked the end of one era and the beginning of another for real estate. It was the end of real estate, as we knew it.

The Federal Reserve System (the Fed) reacted to this crisis by shutting off most bank and savings and loan funding of real estate development between 1990 and 1992. The lending ban on the industry severely limited construction. In response, the Urban Land Institute set up the Real Estate Credit Task Force to work with the Fed to lift the ban.

According to ULI member Bob Larson, a senior executive with Lazard LLC, but at the time a senior member of Taubman Centers management and a member of the task force, the reaction of the Fed to the Real Estate Credit Task Force was "We know the real estate industry is huge, but we know very little about it. Put together some economic information about its impact on the economy." Amazingly, the Fed was aware neither of the actual size of the real estate industry nor of the importance of the industry to the economy.

Recapitalizing the real estate industry required getting the financial faucet turned back on, allowing banks to lend to the industry again. However, the Fed needed an oversight mechanism for this huge industry before it would allow lending to resume. This job of oversight was taken over by Wall Street investment banks, the long-time source of investment and debt financing for major corporations, and the managers of the publicly traded financial markets.

A major problem for real estate has always been that it is an illiquid asset class. Another problem for Wall Street was that real estate was generally owned—by Wall Street standards—in relatively small pieces. Investment bankers got over their hesitancy about real estate by dusting off the old tax category known as real estate investment trusts (REITs). Each publicly traded REIT owns a bundle of real estate assets, valued in the hundreds of millions of dollars initially, that share-owners can buy and sell on a daily basis through a stock exchange—generally the New York Stock Exchange—thus providing liquidity to real estate ownership.

Investment bankers began a binge of initial public offerings of REITs in 1993, when more than 80 were launched. Wall Street firms also got into the trading of commercial mortgage-backed securities (CMBS) bonds for real estate debt in the early 1990s. The new CMBS market came on the heels of Wall Street getting into the secondary residential mortgage business in the late 1980s.

Public markets have a precondition when they agree to trade a company or a product: the public market can only trade "like for like." The market does not want to trade unique things; Wall Street is not an art auction house. When Wall Street took on real estate in the form of REITs and CMBSs in the early 1990s, the real estate industry had to commoditize what it built. Wall Street ended up commoditizing what the industry was building in the 1990s: low-density, car-oriented suburban products. This commoditization resulted in what are referred to as the 19 standard real estate product types, which include entry-level housing subdivisions, suburban garden apartments, warehouses, suburban office parks, and so forth (see chart below).

19 STANDARD REAL ESTATE PRODUCT TYPES

OFFICE
- Build to Suit
- Suburban/Urban Speculation
- Professional/Medical

RENTAL APARTMENT
- Suburban Garden
- Urban High Density

INDUSTRIAL
- Build to Suit
- Warehouse
- Flex/R&D

MISCELLANEOUS
- Self Storage
- Manufactured Housing

RETAIL
- Neighborhood/ Community Center
- Power Center/ Big Box
- Lifestyle/ Town Center

FOR-SALE HOUSING
- Entry Level
- Move-Up
- Luxury
- Active Adult/Retirement
- Resort/Second Home

HOTEL
- Business and Luxury

As of 2007, the 19 standard product types shown in figure 1 are the conforming product types in which investment bankers, lenders, and investors are comfortable investing, because of their track record and known financial performance. Most of these products tend to be drivable and suburban in nature: stand-alone, simple to build, car oriented, and segregated from other uses. Any deviation from these product types was considered nonconforming, and financing nonconforming projects became either impossible or far more expensive.

The real estate industry became more specialized and disciplined starting in the early 1990s. Strategically, large publicly traded companies "stuck to their knitting" by focusing on only one real estate product type. The chief executive officer of a national regional mall company, which had a subsidiary that performed general contracting services for its own malls, was informed by Wall Street analysts that the company should only be developing and managing its malls; general contracting was a diversion. Every company had to have a formal strategic planning process, a human resources department, and financial reporting according to generally accepted standards; public companies were filing required reports with the Securities and Exchange Commission (SEC). Even privately held companies became more disciplined and focused, toeing a much more rigid line because of the higher standards demanded by their bankers and investors.

The growth strategy of many real estate companies began to take the form of what the first edition of this book referred to as "same product/new geographic market"; that is, finding the right location for one of the 19 standard products that could be dropped into a well-understood market segment. For example, the product could be a supermarket-anchored retail center on a 12- to 15-acre site, with a 20 percent coverage ratio, that was set back from the street with plenty of parking for customers to see as they drove past on an arterial that had a minimum of 25,000 cars per day. Making this formula work was merely a matter of finding the right demographics, traffic counts, and size of parcel. Similar formulas were developed for each standard product type.

By the end of 2006 REITs had a market capitalization of $438 billion, CMBSs were a $721 billion market, and the secondary residential mortgage market was $9.2 trillion. REITs now constitute approximately 14 percent of all real estate capital sources, according to Roulac Global Places, LLC. The amount of the market controlled by the ten largest homebuilders (all public companies) rose from

7.56 percent in 1985 to 20.97 percent in 2005. Wall Street no longer considered real estate to be chump change. Real estate had become the fourth major financial asset class, joining the three basics: cash, stock, and bonds.

As a result of these changes to real estate finance, the big real estate companies are only getting bigger. As an industry, real estate has been consolidating and its management systems have been becoming increasingly sophisticated. Real estate has evolved from a locally financed industry to one that is now part of the worldwide finance system. Today, real estate—all publicly traded and privately owned commercial, corporate, and residential real estate in the United States—makes up more than 30 percent of the nation's assets. That is more than all of the publicly traded and private non–real estate companies combined. It is larger than any other asset class in the economy.

This new knowledge allowed the Fed to use the industry, particularly the huge residential sector, to minimize the economic damage caused by the high-tech bust in the first decade of the 21st century. Real estate cushioned the effects of this massive drop in stock market valuation by acting as the locomotive for the entire economy, as did historically low interest rates from a global savings glut.

All these changes have occurred since the publication of the first version of *Strategic Planning for Real Estate Companies*. Now, there are even more fundamental changes to consider, but this time they are happening on the product and marketing side of the industry rather than the finance side.

The Changing Nature of the Real Estate Market

As this book was being written, the for-sale residential real estate sector is in the midst of its first downturn since the early 1990s. The last 15 or so years have been the longest period of real estate growth over the past three generations—maybe the longest ever. All good things must come to an end. Yet the discipline demanded by Wall Street may have kept the great real estate nemesis, overbuilding, at bay this time around, at least compared with previous cycles.

There are indications, however, that the market is changing structurally as well as cyclically. Just as we got really good at building the same suburban, car-oriented product over and over again across the country, there are indications that the market is beginning to demand something different.

Signs that the market has been structurally changing include the following:

■ Popular culture, as seen though movies and television shows, began to glamorize cities and city life in the 1990s and the early years of the 21st century. Shows like *Sex and the City*, *Seinfeld*, and *Friends* portrayed cities as an entirely different kind of place than the dangerous and hopeless settings portrayed in the 1980s (remember *Blade Runner*, *Fort Apache the Bronx*, and *Hill Street Blues*?). There was reality in this changing perception; crime plummeted across the country, making parts of many cities safer than they had been in years.

■ Antigrowth sentiment reached historically high levels in metropolitan areas across the country, especially in the suburbs. Neighborhood groups learned that stopping development was far easier than doing development.

■ The rise of the new urbanism movement and the importance of 24-hour cities, initially promoted by urban planners and architects, gathered steam as city planners, elected officials, and developers began to see the benefits of building higher-density, walkable communities with a mix of uses.

■ Many downtowns unexpectedly began to be redeveloped in the 1990s and the beginning of the 21st century as successful urban entertainment and residential districts. Sometimes their office markets became economically healthier as well. As of 2005 or so, sales and rental rates in these urban districts generally were the highest in their market areas, something no one would have guessed a decade ago.

■ Consumer research in the beginning and middle of the first decade of the 21st century revealed that between 30 and 40 percent of households would prefer a mixed-use, walkable lifestyle to the standard suburban drivable lifestyle. On the supply side, only 5 to 20 percent of the existing residential product is in walkable urban locations, which means there could be considerable pent-up demand for this pattern of development.

■ Mainstream real estate developers—including some of the largest in the country—began to experiment with the development of walkable urban products. Lifestyle centers emerged as an alternative to the regional mall, and two-thirds of the lifestyle centers being planned toward the end of the first decade of the 21st century will contain a mix of uses, typically with housing above retail, according to a Brookings Institution survey. Many of the largest national homebuilders have started urban, high-density divisions, and some of the largest developers in the country, including Related and Forest City Enterprises, focus much of their new development in mixed-use, walkable urban projects.

■ Finally, concern about climate change has reached critical mass. The intuitive connection between low-density, drivable suburban development patterns and greenhouse gas emissions is clear. While public policy regarding climate change has not yet changed, it no doubt will.

The real estate strategies created to develop and manage a commoditized, drivable suburban world are beginning to look out of date. It is unusual for the real estate industry—which adds only about 2 percent to its asset base annually—to fundamentally change its product offerings. Still, the potential pent-up demand for alternatives to the 19 standard product types is being noticed. But making such a change will not be easy.

The major difference between the appropriate real estate strategies of the 1990s and today is that the former were product-specialized (same product, new markets) and the latter have become much more place-based. Although it once was relatively simple for developers to build specialized products in suburban greenfield locations, the demand for walkable urban places is proving to be much more difficult to satisfy. Walkable urban developments need a critical mass of development—which could include residential, entertainment, employment, retail, cultural, and educational uses—all within walking distance of one another. A walkable place that accommodates all these different land uses will be between 200 and 500 acres in size, or two to five times the size of a regional mall, including its surface parking lot. Developers can get to this critical mass by slowly building the pieces over time; in essence, promoting the walkable urban excitement that will be here soon, if you just wait. This is not a great marketing platform. Or they can develop enough products in the first phase to achieve critical mass immediately, as developers did at Atlantic Station in Atlanta, Belmar in suburban Denver, and Reston Town Center in the Virginia suburbs of Washington, D.C. But this is a risky proposition.

Walkable urbanism is a far more complex development pattern than the drivable suburban pattern that most of the real estate industry is skilled at planning, designing, developing, and operating. It also is new to the financial community, which means that, as of this writing, Wall Street investment houses have been hesitant to see publicly traded firms get into this kind of development. Most of the early adopters have been smaller private companies.

Developing walkable urban projects requires completing a significant amount of planning, infrastructure, zoning, and marketing work early in the process, before substantial development takes place. This early work, known as "place making," requires much more upfront investment and—generally—significant public involvement. The infrastructure required is entirely different than that needed by the drivable suburban development of the past 50 years and typically includes some form of transit or other transportation alternatives to driving.

Planning, designing, developing, and operating mixed-use projects also is much more complex. Each additional product type (housing, office, retail, and so forth) adds to a project's market exposure and risk. Yet interesting and profitable relationships among different product types—such as the relationship between for-sale condominiums and a hotel in a mixed-use project—can benefit both real estate companies and the project's ultimate users.

It is important to note that not every project in a walkable urban place will be mixed use. There still will be plenty of opportunities for real estate companies that specialize in single product types like office or apartment buildings. But even these companies may need to learn how to include other uses (small amounts of ground-floor retail space, for instance) in their projects, and they must learn to work within a new mixed-use environment.

The Need for Strategic Balance

One thing has not changed: real estate is still a cyclical business. Over the past half-century, when the economy caught a cold, the real estate industry caught pneumonia and some real estate companies died. While increased Wall Street scrutiny and Federal Reserve discipline may have lessened the cyclicality of the industry, one would be foolish to assume it is a stable business. The same basic issues of high capital costs, long lead times, and customers having to make large purchase or lease decisions that could be postponed if economic or consumer confidence condition change makes for a volatile business. A pipeline of under-construction and planned projects that can be three years long could face declining consumer demand literally overnight, leading to that worst of all market situations, overbuilding, which can take years to burn off.

We currently are in the middle of a definite slowdown in the for-sale housing market, after a ten- to 12-year expansion. It is certainly possible that various income products, such as apartments or office, could follow. This will require companies to "batten down the hatches"—in some cases for the first time in half a generation. It could lead to real estate companies laying off employees, closing offices, shifting from development to asset management, shedding land, and so forth.

Although it may sound masochistic, real estate downturns can be healthy. They force all companies in the industry to reevaluate their strategies, make decisions about issues that they did not have to face in good times, get out of businesses and markets that do not have as much potential as others, become more efficient, and take other courses of action that—while painful in the short term—will be beneficial in the long term. In particular, downturns provide great opportunities for companies that are well positioned to take advantage of the pain of others. In retrospect, the bargains that many real estate companies and investors picked up in the early 1990s, especially the sale of assets from the Resolution Trust Corporation, proved to be the foundation of their success for much of the subsequent upturn. The Toll Brothers and Lennar homebuilding operations, for example, purchased what at the time looked like very risky land at 20 to 40 cents on the dollar from its previous peak values, positioning the company for one of the great success stories of the era.

To take advantage of the upturn, however, a company must be alive. "Calling" the end of a cyclical upturn and shifting strategies to a more defensive, survival-oriented approach is the most important decision a company can make. A company that misses a cyclical upturn by a year or so will lose out on some opportunities by being too late. But missing the adjustment from an expanding market to a contracting one can be fatal. This may be especially true in 2008 and beyond, because the last downturn was so long ago that many young companies and their leaders have experienced only good times. These firms are particularly vulnerable to missing the turn and going off the road.

Strategic planning for real estate companies thus is more important than ever. Wall Street, investors, and banks all demand it but, even more important, the marketplace demands it. When the marketplace is changing both cyclically and structurally, real estate executives face too many uncertainties to not have a clear picture of where their company is going. Responding to both types of market changes will require fundamental changes in a company's financial, organizational, and marketing structures and approaches. Both types of changes will require company leaders to make difficult decisions, some of which will take the company in directions it has never gone in the past.

These cyclical and structural changes and the complexity they imply are the reasons why real estate companies need strategic planning. In a capital-intensive business, in which the consequences of poor decision making may not be known for years to come, strategic planning becomes even more important.

Christopher B. Leinberger
Visiting Fellow, The Brookings Institution
Director/Professor of Graduate Real Estate Program, University of Michigan
Partner in Arcadia Land Company

CHAPTER 1

The Need for a Strategy

Every company has a strategy. The question is whether the strategy is explicit—the result of careful planning, born out of a consensus among the company's top leadership—or implicit—an unconscious decision to keep on doing what the company has been doing and simply muddle through. Many real estate firms follow the latter course.

This book is an introduction to strategic planning for all types of real estate companies—large and small, private and public, those that are focused on a narrow set of geographies or products and those that are fully diversified, multi-disciplined concerns. It is a primer on the most important issues managers face: how to set the direction of the firm and implement an action plan to ensure that the strategy is pursued.

Strategic planning is an intellectual-sounding name for a deceptively simple process: determining where a business is going and how it plans to get there. Especially at a time when the real estate industry is rapidly changing and consolidating, it is important to define company goals in both absolute and relative terms and to tie goals to specific strategies. Without this important step, strategic planning becomes only an empty exercise that does not achieve any goal.

It is important to demystify strategic planning. It is not a black box or a magic bullet. It involves determining what senior managers want a company to be when it grows to the next level—and then figuring out how to get there. Asking where the company wants to go and how to get there every few years is a healthy exercise, one that is essential when times are uncertain but equally important as conditions improve. The most successful companies regularly monitor economic and real estate market cycles, and revisit and adjust their strategies accordingly.

Companies with well-defined strategic plans and a well-defined business strategy are at a distinct advantage: they have a common direction that is clear to all. For publicly traded companies, the market has spoken; those with a clear focus and a well-articulated strategy tend to garner a premium from analysts and shareholders. For all real estate companies, a strategic plan and the planning process itself offer a competitive edge, enabling the company to focus its talents and energies and to measure achievements against expectations.

Some examples:

■ In the early 1990s, the northeast and mid-Atlantic partners of a national multifamily company were having a difficult time raising capital to fund their development activities, a frustrating experience in the face of seemingly favorable market fundamentals. They decided to turn to Wall Street for capital and formed a real estate investment trust (REIT) in 1993. Later, as they discovered that the company was not able to grow organically as quickly as they had hoped, the firm's leaders decided that the best path to growth lay in a merger with a California-based multifamily REIT that had similar strategies and complementary strengths. During the recession of the early part of the first decade of the 21st century, the merged firm remained true to its market strategy (Class A, high barriers to entry), repurchased stock, slowed its development pipeline, and sold assets to keep its balance sheet strong and position itself for growth during the next upturn. The company emerged from the recession as an industry leader with a robust development pipeline.

■ A private, regional residential real estate firm noted that its competitors seemed to be more successful in generating wealth for their principals despite operating at a scale similar to its own but without the same high level of market awareness and risk. Why, the company's leaders wondered, were others taking fewer risks and making more money while they seemed to be paying what they felt was too much for capital while still providing loan guarantees personally? After evaluating what their firm did best, they recognized that they had been unnecessarily "giving away" their valuable presence in the market and their recognizable brand, which was able to generate premium pricing and occupancy for their equity partners. They also realized that by broadening their joint venture strategy, they could become an equity partner in deals in return for their sweat equity, and that they needed to work harder to find the right equity sources and partners. In 2007, the company formed a joint venture with an institutional investor that has enabled it to grow and expand into new markets, increasing the partners' equity stake in a much larger portfolio while reducing their financial exposure.

■ A Texas-based development firm that built 5 million square feet of office and industrial space in Austin, Dallas, and Houston found itself in crisis as the state's energy-dominated economy cratered in the early 1980s. Faced with a hemorrhaging balance sheet and no prospects for development in its core markets for some time, the company embarked upon a transition into a third-party management, leasing, transaction, and investment sales business. The firm experienced tremendous growth during the 1980s and 1990s, merging with and acquiring other companies to become a national provider of real estate services, including research and tenant advisory services. Having successfully transformed the company into one of the nation's preeminent service companies, the principals felt they were missing out on development opportunities and that they could effectively leverage the company's service platform, parlaying it into development deals, and vice versa. In 2007, the firm had a $500 million development pipeline, and its principals are wrestling with how to best integrate development capabilities into a large service-based organization in order to continue the firm's legacy as an evergreen company.

■ In the early 1980s, a second-generation, family-owned local homebuilding company found itself struggling in the midst of the housing downturn. It turned out that its profits came from its horizontal land development activities, while its core vertical homebuilding business was losing money. The solution was quite simple: sell the homebuilding business, along with a long-term contract to continue providing finished lots, to a large national builder that was interested in penetrating the market. The company then reinvested the proceeds, evolving into a regional, multidisciplined real estate company with commercial, retail, and industrial land and vertical building capabilities, rental apartments, general contracting, and—after its noncompetitive agreement burned off—a homebuilding business. By the late 1990s, with no obvious heir apparent, the family patriarch decided it was time to make a transition from family to professional management, with the objectives of continuing to grow the business and securing the company's legacy. The firm's new chief executive officer (CEO) examined the company business by business to determine their relative profitability. By 2007, the company had shed certain businesses, become more sophisticated in its use and redeployment of capital, partnered with other successful industry players in increasingly larger projects, and was actively acquiring, developing, and managing a diverse range of real estate products throughout the southeastern United States and beyond.

These are just four examples of real estate companies that have faced strategic challenges at crucial points in the economic and real estate market cycle. Each company needed to determine its future direction and how it planned to get there. All of them needed strategies to guide this process.

Planning Is Invaluable

As General Dwight D. Eisenhower once said, "Plans are useless, but planning is indispensable." No matter how much effort and thought a company puts into a strategic planning process, the plan will never precisely forecast what will happen to that company. However, no matter how imperfect the plan, the planning process will define the upside potential and the downside risks that the company faces, enabling it to build capacity to deal with known external opportunities and threats as well as to keep the company flexible enough to handle unanticipated opportunities and threats, while forging a conscious consensus among top managers regarding the direction of the company. The conscious consensus among managers is the most important outcome of the strategic planning process.

Strategic planning should aim to define the company's future direction, focusing on opportunities, considering its internal and external realities, its history, its people, and the realities of capital, the marketplace, and other factors. Even if top managers already have a fairly good idea of the direction in which the company should be headed, they can benefit from a strategic planning process that tests hypotheses, explores more specific potentialities, and provides input—and creates buy-in—from the key players in the organization who will be charged with implementing the strategy. The process should take a fresh look at the company, its products or services, and the market to define a new vision for the firm or potentially chart a new course.

The time frame encompassed by a strategic plan varies from company to company, depending on the financial condition of the organization, the economic outlook of the industry, and company executives' experience with strategy. Typically, a strategic plan should look out over a three- to five-year horizon, because this typically has been the time frame in which the real estate market shifts from one phase of the cycle to another: from upturn to maturity, or downturn to recovery, and so forth. It is true that some real estate expansion periods last longer than others, but companies are well served if they revisit their strategy over each phase of the cycle. For some, this revisit simply confirms their plans, but for others it provides an opportunity to fine-tune, adjust, and question what they should do differently during the extended cycle, as well as when the real estate economy changes.

Forest City Enterprises, Inc., is a company that agrees planning is valuable. As its mission statement highlights, the company "operates with a consistent focus on its strategic plan. The strategy is clear: We focus on target markets with high growth potential and where we enjoy distinct competitive advantages."

The Real Estate Cycle: Why Planning Is Particularly Important for Real Estate Companies

Real estate is one of the largest segments of the national economy. Recent work by Dr. Stephen Roulac estimates that the entire asset base in the United States is valued at $200 trillion; that is what it would take to buy the country. Real estate, broadly defined, represents 35 percent of that asset value and, at approximately $90 trillion, is the single largest asset class in the country (figure 1-1).

Real estate also is one of the most cyclical industries in the economy. Real estate experiences higher highs and lower lows than most other industries, including the automobile, aerospace, energy, and other highly cyclical industries. Even more important, a moderation of growth in the overall economy can cause a recession in real estate, particularly if there is a rapid erosion of consumer confidence or a change in capital market liquidity, the lifeblood of real estate. As the saying goes, "When the economy catches a cold, the real estate industry contracts pneumonia."

Figure 1-1: UNITED STATES ASSET BASE

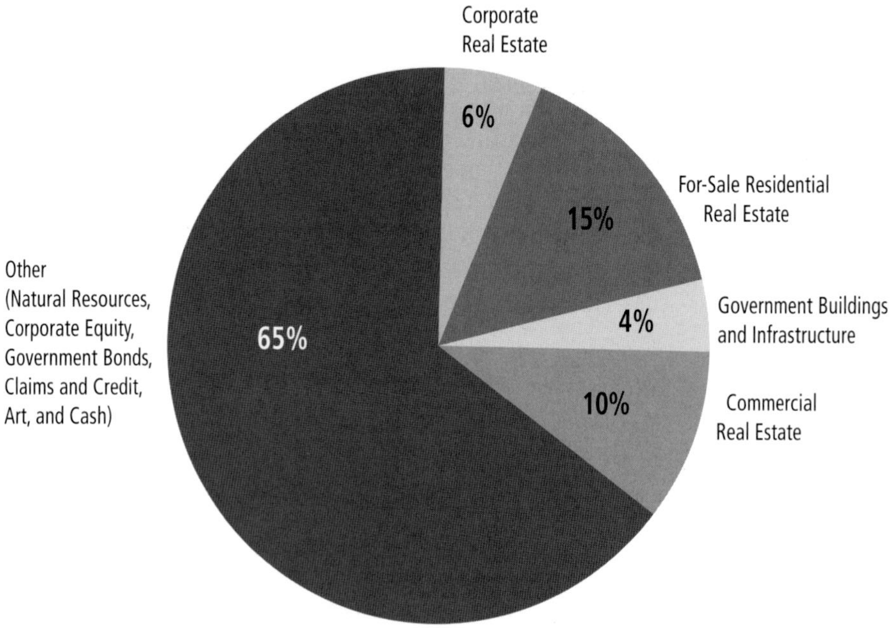

Source: Roulac Global Places, LLC.

More than any other factor, the reaction of industry players to the real estate cycle determines what the strategy of a real estate company should be. When formulating a strategy, a company therefore must start with an understanding of the effects of these extreme cycles. To ignore the extreme cyclical nature of the industry is to place a company in peril, dooming it to continuous crisis during every real estate depression. If companies do not plan adequately for deep downturns, they will never survive to enjoy the inevitable upturns.

Most real estate veterans would say that they know that real estate is cyclical. But the unusually long run that real estate experienced in the 1990s and from 2000 through 2005 seems to have made many in the industry forget this reality—or at least not plan adequately for the cycle's eventual turn, particularly in the residential sector. No one who was working for a homebuilding company in 2006 and 2007 is likely to forget for quite some time that real estate is a cyclical business.

The real estate cycle comprises three general phases, as shown in figure 1-2 and described below.

Upturn Phase

This phase typically lasts one to two years. In its early stages, most sectors remain in a "buyer's market," as smart buyers recognize that this period—when many sellers still have a downturn mentality—is a good time to buy. Most buyers remain cautious; they are not even sure an upturn has begun. Once vacancies fall into a reasonable range in response to general economic recovery, however, the usual result is rising demand for space and apartments. Yet the lead time required for developers to respond to this demand is too long to produce the new space or units that are needed. Consequently, as the upturn continues, managers allow rents of existing space or units to rise while they reduce or eliminate concessions. Homebuilders are able to obtain higher—in some cases, much higher—prices for their products. The appetite for investment tends to be strong during this phase, further driving property values up.

Mature Phase

Although the real estate industry has just experienced a historically long period of expansion, the mature phase typically lasts for one to three years. The mature phase is a time of approximate equilibrium. Property owners must be willing to sell into the mature phase; those trying to catch the peak of the cycle may miss it. Toward the end of the mature phase, however, an increasing amount of new space and an excess inventory of rental apartments and for-sale homes typically

Figure 1-2: REAL ESTATE CYCLE

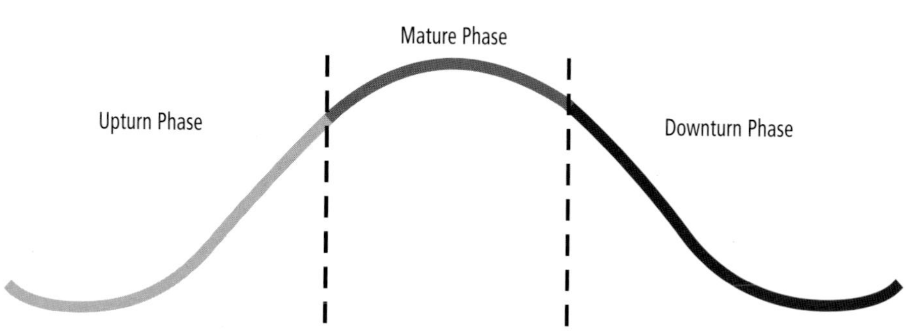

come onto the market, causing a shift, virtually overnight, to a buyer's market. The increased supply forces homebuilders to lower prices and owners to lower rents and increase concessions. Despite rising vacancies and falling rents, unduly optimistic projections about the future performance of new projects generally keeps the pipeline full of additional new inventory, unless financial institutions and investors demand increased preleasing and more conservative absorption and rental rate assumptions in the pro formas. Property values are the last to soften in the mature phase.

Downturn Phase

Usually lasting from two to four years—although some markets have experienced much longer downturns (witness Houston in the 1980s, Los Angeles in the 1990s, and, perhaps, Detroit in the first decade of the 21st century)—the downturn is a period of adjustment. Falling demand and excess capacity force drastic concessions, lower rents, lower home prices, and lower values. The result is the bankruptcy of marginal projects and companies and a serious decline in the financial performance of nearly every company and project in the market. Land prices are typically the last in the industry to get adjusted to new market realities, but these, too, eventually are brought down by sagging demand. The bankruptcy of developers, coupled with unduly pessimistic demand projections by financial institutions and investors hurt by the downturn, limits the development of any new product well beyond the period of the downturn, thus setting the foundation for the next upturn.

Historically, both undue optimism and undue pessimism have been major factors in the extremely cyclical nature of the real estate industry. In the early 1990s, for example, many industry observers and participants predicted a paralysis in the industry for years to come. Yet the long-dormant REIT vehicle created much-needed liquidity at a time when many companies were struggling to stay afloat. Recall Sam Zell's often-quoted mantra from the early years of the 21st century: "Stay alive to [20]05!"

On the other side of the coin, during the for-sale housing boom that lasted through 2005 or so, many believed that the good times would never end. Speculative fever in the homebuilding sector, particularly in condominiums, was driven by the view that real estate was a sure bet: Investors and, by extension, developers cannot lose, cycles have been banished from the markets; this is the dawn of a new era! The for-sale housing bubble burst loudly in 2005—although many did not hear the pop until some time in 2006—just as the tech bubble had burst earlier in the same decade. Worth noting: real estate is still an extremely cyclical business.

Reacting to Trends and Cyclicality

Such irrational exuberance (thank you, Alan Greenspan, for nailing the term) or pessimism is almost always misplaced. Markets always correct themselves on both the downside and the upside as supply and demand return to balance. The form of the industry may change over time, as may the sources and mechanisms of financing and the structure of the companies within the industry. But the ever-changing U.S. and global economies and the continually transforming size and shape of our metropolitan areas—not to mention the continued obsolescence of older buildings and locations as well as the growth of the U.S. population by 3 million people and 1.4 million households per year—are guarantees. The industry will always emerge from downturns eventually, no matter how devastating they are. We are fortunate in the United States—structural demand always returns.

REASONS FOR CYCLICALITY IN REAL ESTATE

- Fixed and variable costs
- Long-term commitment and consumer confidence
- Long lead times for new product
- Irrational exuberance

Many factors contribute to the real estate industry's extreme overreaction to economic trends. They are described in the following sections.

Fixed and Variable Costs

The relationship between fixed and variable costs is one of the primary reasons for the extreme cyclical nature of the industry. The fixed costs of a leveraged new development account for approximately 70 percent of break-even revenues. In other words, the debt service for a new project represents most of that project's costs, assuming the project breaks even. The variable costs associated with running the project, including property management, maintenance, utilities, and taxes, amount to only about 30 percent of break-even revenues. During a downturn, when the market is overbuilt, it makes short-term economic sense to price space well below the break-even point. Owners should, however, keep lease terms short so that they do not lock in low rates for the long term. Conversely, firms can realize generally high rents and occupancy rates during the upturn phase of the cycle, and thus considerable profits. Once the break-even point is reached, 70 percent of every dollar of rent drops to the bottom line.

This is analogous to what happens in the airline business, and the relationship between fixed and variable costs is very similar at 30 to 70 percent. When times are tough, airlines drop fares to induce more customers to fly—often well below the 30 percent break-even point. When this is not sufficient, airlines attempt to cut capacity in an effort to gain pricing power and cut costs, although this is difficult to do with powerful labor unions. In real estate, it is not possible to mothball a bunch of rental apartments or an office building to gain pricing power and better balance the demand/supply equation. Those units and unleased space are going nowhere, and owners simply must wait for the demand to catch up to the supply and return to equilibrium.

Long-Term Commitment and Consumer Confidence

The second factor that affects the industry's overreaction to economic trends is the long-term customer commitment required by most real estate products and, more specifically, how good or bad that customer is feeling about the future when it is time to make a long-term commitment. For example, the typical office lease is for five years; many are for ten years or longer. When a company's lease comes due during an economic downturn, it may be conservative about the amount of space it requires. Such firms typically lease no more space than needed for their current operations and may even shed surplus space, creating a large shadow market in subleased space. As the economy improves, however, businesses become more sanguine about the future. Long-term lease decisions are easier to justify, and companies rent a more generous amount of space for both current use and future expansion.

The same thing happens when individuals decide to rent apartments or purchase homes. If a young person on the verge of minting a brand new household feels good about the prospects of finding gainful employment, he or she likely will sign an apartment lease or a contract to buy a home. In an economic downturn, however, many of these young people will decide not to form households or will double and triple up instead of occupying their own space, thereby creating far fewer net new households. Concessions to attract new renters and purchasers often are matched or bettered by the competition, and the buyer's market is suddenly going full force.

Long Lead Time for New Product

A third reason for the industry's extreme overreaction to economic trends is the increasingly long lead time required to bring new space and new housing developments on line. The transition from too little space to too much space can occur almost overnight through a change in perception of the market reality. At the beginning of a downturn, after the emergence of a buyer's or a tenant's market, many projects already in the development pipeline will proceed regardless of events. This is because it can take two or more years to complete a major project, such as a hotel, office building, or apartment complex. The pipeline therefore will dump a significant amount of product on the buyer's market when it is least needed or wanted.

The same lead-time factor works during an upturn. Once a seller's market returns, with improving consumer confidence, declining vacancies, and increasing rents, developers need the same two to three years to deliver new products to the market. The delivery time for some real estate products, such as for-sale housing and industrial space, can be much shorter, so the ability of the market to respond to spikes in demand can be enhanced to some degree. Developers who wait to start a new project until the seller's market is evident may find that by the time the project is delivered two or three years later, the cycle has turned and the project faces a buyer's market. This is particularly true for large-scale and multiphase projects.

Irrational Exuberance

The fourth reason for the extremely cyclical nature of the industry is the unbridled optimism of developers and investors who, even in the face of significant overbuilding, often decide to go ahead with new projects that were begun during the mature phase of the cycle and do not have adequate market support. Much has been made of the impact that increased scrutiny from Wall Street and global capital markets has made on the real estate industry. Industry observers argue that more information and increased transparency prevent the kind of overbuilding that we have seen in the past because of the increased discipline imposed by the capital markets. While it is true that more information is available to investors and developers than ever before, it is perhaps too soon to declare the patient cured.

Developers and their investment partners continue to be lulled by the strength of the market during cycle upswings, and extremely high levels of capital continue flooding into real estate—that is, until the crash comes. Can single-digit capitalization rates for income-producing properties be justified, given the risk inherent in such a cyclical business, even in periods of relatively low inflation? Many of those making the big decisions about financing real estate acquisitions and investments have never been through a downturn. In light of this, can we say that the culture of unbridled optimism in the real estate industry is truly over? If ten office projects or ten apartment communities are in the planning stages in a given market, and all are underwritten on the assumption that they will capture 20 percent of the demand in that market, then all of them will suffer when they are put into production—even if the demand remains constant or increases, which is not what happens when the market enters a downturn. Even when the market does not want new development, developers and investors tend to ignore reality, rationalize, and build anyway.

In the preparation of a strategic plan, it is crucial to identify both the current phase of the cycle and the phase likely to characterize the next several years. A realistic assessment of the market is essential to developing an appropriate, optimal strategy. Since 20/20 forward vision does not exist in the real estate industry, it is essential to determine strategies to deal with changes and unforeseen events.

Real Estate Company Dimensions

Real estate companies of all shapes and sizes can benefit from strategic planning. Real estate companies can often be defined by looking at the seven key dimensions, highlighted in the accompanying box.

A structural change in the types of real estate companies—from place-based real estate companies and organizations to specialized, product-based companies driven by Wall Street—began to take place in the 1990s. Another structural shift may now be underway with the addition of new standardized products such as walkable urbanity, which may dictate a return to place-based organization structure.

DIMENSIONS OF REAL ESTATE COMPANIES

- Primary activities
- Geography
- Product type
- Capital structure
- Size and scale
- Structural change
- Structural shift

Why Real Estate Companies Plan

While it could certainly be argued that every real estate concern should undertake some level of strategic planning, regardless of its size or situation, real estate companies tend to engage in strategic planning efforts when they are faced with certain catalytic events.

CAUSES FOR STRATEGIC PLANING

- Changing economic and real estate environments
- Changes in ownership or leadership
- Mergers and acquisitions
- Tremendous growth
- Challenges to growth
- Legacy vision

Changing Economic and Real Estate Environments

A looming shift from one phase of the real estate cycle to the next—or the realization that one already has occurred—typically can trigger management to revisit and potentially alter a company's strategy. For example, the Artery Group, a private multidisciplined development and asset management firm headquartered in the Washington, D.C., market, learned from its experiences in the down cycle in the late 1980s, when it was slow to recognize the significant real estate cycle shift that took place then. The company was focused on homebuilding, apartments, office, and land development, predominantly in the Washington, D.C., metropolitan area. Early warning signals indicated that Artery was overextended and overleveraged; it had excellent land assets, but the debt service on those land inventories was becoming difficult to sustain. The firm's leaders, however, were in "late stage denial," reluctant to admit that the cycle had moved from one phase to the next. They began to react too late, selling some of the assets but not nearly enough to avoid notable suffering. The cycle was deeper and more painful than anticipated and, as a consequence, Artery lost many of its assets and went through a recapitalization and a difficult adjustment period in the late 1980s and early 1990s.

Between the mid-1990s and 2005, the firm came back quite strongly, building a whole new asset base and a nine-figure net worth. As Artery's leaders began to sense that another down cycle was approaching in 2006, they responded more aggressively and masterfully than before. Recognizing that the market was becoming very frosty, they methodically lightened their balance sheet—this time selling at peak prices—by liquidating most of their assets and resisting the temptation to purchase land and begin new projects outside the Washington, D.C., metropolitan area. As of the third quarter of 2007, they were sitting on a very clean balance sheet, were holding some land that remains highly valuable, and had plenty of cash on hand (or "dry powder") with which they will be able to take advantage of the opportunities that will be presented by other people's mistakes during the next downturn.

Changes in Ownership or Leadership

Any shift in key leadership positions, whether in a family-owned and -operated business or in a public company planning the succession from one owner or leader to the next, can trigger the need for a shift in strategy. At the H.G. Fenton Company, the challenge of the early part of the first decade of the 21st century was how to make an orderly shift from family to professional management. The San Diego–based company, founded in 1906, operated rock, sand, and gravel plants. It evolved into a commercial real estate company in the 1980s, primarily in industrial, value office, and retail space, and expanded into multifamily properties in the late 1990s. The family had the foresight to set up the real estate operation with a very conservative balance sheet structure and, later, to bring in a professional management team. In 2002, H. Fenton Hunte, the founder's grandson, stepped down as president and Mike Neal, who had joined the company in 1988, became its first president and chief operating officer from outside the family.

At the same time, the company went through an open and participatory strategic planning exercise. Family leaders—through Hunte's continuing involvement (as chairman)—set clear, well-defined parameters for what they expected the company to do and how they would measure its success, then gave the professional management team a tremendous amount of autonomy in how it achieved that success. The managers consequently felt empowered, rather than micromanaged. Under Neal's direction, the H.G. Fenton Company, which continues to be family owned, has become one of the largest real estate owners and developers in San Diego County. In 2006, it began expanding its focus to additional California markets while also becoming a third-party provider of capital, debt, and equity to other developers.

Mergers and Acquisitions

Mergers and acquisitions often trigger the desire to question every aspect of a company's strategy and to identify synergies, best practices, and efficiencies that often were the genesis of the transactions. Although in some acquisitions—and even many so-called "mergers of equals"—the larger, stronger, or smarter firm simply transfers its existing strategy to the operations of the acquired firm, mergers and acquisitions can also trigger a new strategic planning process.

The merger of Avalon Properties and Bay Apartment Communities as AvalonBay Communities, however, was a true merger of equals. The firms combined executive offices and boards in what was an unusual and unique situation. The need for strategic planning at the corporate level was driven by the desire to organize the new firm as a merger of equal companies. This was the approach: "Neither your strategy nor my strategy will survive; we will have a new strategy. Neither your organization nor my organization will survive; we will have a new organization." The result was a concerted effort to identify the things that each organization did particularly well and to ensure that those best practices were spread across the platform of the new, combined firm. (See the case study on page 167 for more details.) Even in straightforward acquisitions, the smart acquiring company will optimize the benefits of that acquisition by taking the time to analyze the core competencies of the company it has acquired and trying to integrate those core competencies and best practices into the new, combined organization.

Tremendous Growth

In many cases, an organization's structure and development have not kept pace with changes in the market or expansions in the volume of its activity. Such companies need to consider that the way they have conducted business in the past—indeed, the very structure of the organization—may no longer make sense.

As Trico Homes of Calgary, Alberta, Canada, increased its housing development from building 50 homes per year to building 250 per year, with ambitions to double that number over the next three to five years, it faced organizational and operational challenges. Its leaders knew they had a problem because they were experiencing staff turnover and because they were identifying development opportunities that they were unable to execute. They recognized that they needed to rethink and restructure the organization and consequently began an intensive strategy planning process to question how and where the company should grow and how it should be restructured. The result was a decision to address the challenges created by explosive growth by deepening the company's market penetration of its home market, as well as expanding into additional markets, and to break out its multifamily, single-family, and custom homebuilding activities into separate divisions.

Challenges to Growth

On the other side of the coin, decreasing levels of activity, changes in the competitive environment, or impediments to growth can trigger the need to reinvigorate or reposition, expand, diversify, or possibly rationalize activities, markets, products, or services. For example, the Linpro Company, a national development and investment firm focused primarily on the speculative development of office, industrial, and other commercial properties, hit the skids during the recession of the late 1980s and early 1990s. Its leaders realized they needed to reinvent the company in order to survive.

A core group of Linpro's leaders acquired the firm's assets and re-formed the company as LCOR Incorporated in 1992. (The acquisition maintained Linpro's previous executive alignment, as the lead partners of Linpro became the shareholders of LCOR.) As the firm's history notes, "LCOR was formed to reflect the changing nature of the real estate industry, to address the need for third-party advisory and consulting services in addition to development and investment activities, and to help government agencies and public authorities maximize the value and utility of the vast amount of underutilized real estate owned or controlled by them." The company thus undertook a number of large build-to-suit contracts with the federal government and ultimately morphed into a fee developer and contractor of federal and other public sector businesses. By the late 1990s and the first few years of the 21st century, LCOR began to return to speculative, at-risk development projects for its own account.

Legacy Vision

The desire to develop a well-thought-out strategic plan often stems from the desire to create a long-term vision and lasting legacy, whereby the company can continue to perform in good times and bad and to prosper beyond the current ownership or administration. Ron Terwilliger, chairman and CEO of Trammell Crow Residential (TCR), uses the term "evergreen" to describe his goal for TCR, one of the nation's largest rental apartment companies. "By 'evergreen,'" says Terwilliger, "we mean, among other things, that TCR will endure beyond the business life of any one individual." He also wants the firm to be evergreen by making money during all "seasons": not just when it develops new product and not just when the wind is at its back, but in all phases of the real estate cycle.

A similar example is East West Partners, which grew from a single-market, "everybody does everything" company in the mid-1970s to a large, multimarket residential and resort developer and manager operating primarily in the western United States. By the 1990s, the firm's leaders, partly in recognition of their own mortality (all were entering or in their sixties at the time), realized that they needed to plan for the company's growth more strategically in order to ensure its long-term continuity. Because the expanding organization had taken on about a dozen senior managers in their forties who were not part of the founding group and did not have a common vision, East West Partners engaged those managers in a strategic planning process as both a way to ensure their buy-in to the strategy and a legacy planning exercise. The process worked so well that East West Partners eventually reached even deeper into the organization, involving even more junior and younger managers in the strategic planning process.

Not All Cash Flows Are Created Equal

With the knowledge that cycles have not been banished from the economy—and certainly not from the real estate industry—companies that build an evergreen strategy are the most likely to succeed, both in the near term and over the long haul. To build a balanced strategy, real estate companies must understand the risk implicit in the different sources of cash flow available to the industry. The two basic types of activities in the real estate industry have their own risk/reward profiles. They are capital risk activities, which typically involve investing one's own—equity capital—or that of investors or partners—for real estate development or acquisition, and operating risk activities, which typically involve fee income activities that put only the company's working capital at risk. These are discussed in more detail in chapter 3.

SOURCES OF CASH FLOW

- Long-term asset income
- Service business income
- Capital risk fee income
- Capital risk transaction income
- Long-term asset sales

Some sources of cash flow are inherently more risky than others because of their expected performance during the three phases of the real estate cycle. Only five internally generated sources of cash flow are available to a real estate company. The five sources listed below can be ranked in order of highest to lowest quality, or consistency. The highest-quality sources are less likely to be affected by a downturn, whereas the lower-quality sources are more likely to evaporate during difficult times.

■ *Long-Term Asset Income,* which may be defined as cash-flowing, underleveraged, or low-leverage owned assets such as leased income property and cash or cash equivalents. These assets, which often constitute the heart of a company's portfolio, are expected to help the firm survive downturns and build net worth over the long term. That is not to say that these assets should never be sold or recapitalized. In fact, long-term asset holders should actively manage the assets to optimize the portfolio's risk-adjusted return, and this very often means that there are times to sell, times to hold, and times to buy.

■ *Service Business Income,* which consists of net revenue from service businesses such as property management fees, portfolio and asset management fees, workout and consulting fees, and maintenance service fees. Although these revenue streams can decline during a downturn, properties still need to be maintained and serviced in good times and bad, and typically, there is some level of predictable income. Furthermore, in a downturn, institutional investors need assistance with workouts. As a consequence, these revenues are expected to help the firm weather downturns and build its long-term foundation.

■ *Capital Risk Fee Income,* which can be defined as revenues generated when the firm pursues capital risk activity, includes income such as acquisition fees, development fees, and disposition fees from land development, building development, acquisition or repositioning of an existing building, and the like. This short-term revenue typically is generated only when the company or its financial partners assume substantial long-term risk; such revenue is less available during the downturn phase of the cycle than during the upturn and mature phases.

■ *Capital Risk Transaction Income* may be defined as profits from the sale of capital risk assets that were developed or acquired for repositioning and intended to be sold. It is difficult to take advantage of this source of cash flow during downturns.

■ *Long-Term Asset Sales* result in profits from the sale or the leveraging of cash-flowing owned assets. This source of cash flow is comparable to the manager of a trust or endowment dipping into the principal: it should be avoided if at all possible to ensure that the highest-quality source of cash flow, long-term asset income, remains intact. In a sense, this is an example of culling the goose that lays the golden eggs.

Externally generated sources of cash flow for real estate companies (as distinct from real estate assets) typically are limited to private investors—most often the owners or principals of the firm—and Wall Street, through the issuance of public shares or through private equity funds (discussed further in chapter 9). Contrary to early popular belief, publicly traded real estate companies, principally large national homebuilders and REITs, are indeed subject to the same "quality of cash flow" principles listed above. It can be challenging for these companies to raise capital through additional public equity or debt offerings when the market is experiencing a downturn. Institutional investors, private equity firms, and pension funds play a critical role as sources of funding for real estate development and acquisition. These investors, however, rarely invest discretely and selectively in real estate companies; instead, they invest generally in bundles of assets.

During the upturn and mature phases of the real estate cycle, many development companies become addicted to cash flow from capital risk fees and capital risk transactions. When the markets turn down, as they inevitably do, development activity dries up and with it the income generated from these activities. This is the phase of the cycle when income from long-term assets and from service businesses is desired. Those who do not have such income suffer a rude awakening as they scramble to restructure their cost structure, lay off their development staffs, and start searching for alternative sources of income. Those who fail to restructure or enter service businesses risk going out of business or continuing on as mere shadows of their former selves. At the other end of the spectrum, those who realize the value of a more balanced approach always place considerable emphasis on long-term asset income and service business cash flow and, as a result, fare much better during the downturn and survive to benefit from the next upturn.

The value of strategic balance has recast the premises on which development companies are based. As recently as the early 1990s, it became clear that most development companies could no longer survive by limiting their pursuits to development activities. Many of the companies that once saw themselves as development companies now view themselves as real estate companies that achieve strategic balance by combining capital risk activities with operating risk businesses. By considering all capital risk and operating risk roles, a company can balance its strategic risk and open itself to many more opportunities. Of course, defining a company as a real estate company rather than a development company is easier said than done.

The Universe of Strategic Options

When the top managers of a development company decide that it should become a balanced real estate company, a few central questions loom large. What are the defining characteristics of the company, and what are the areas in which the company can excel? Who are the company's customers, and how can it differentiate itself in an often crowded development and investment marketplace? What are the best roles for a given company, and how does a firm determine which options best serve its needs? How can the company operate efficiently and effectively in pursuit of its vision and business objectives? How is it going to finance its vision and ambition? And how is it going to insulate itself from the bad things that happen even to good companies when the market turns down? These are the questions that strategic planning is designed to answer.

What, Not *How*

Strategies are the means by which a company accomplishes its goals. They provide a framework for establishing the actions that will be taken on a day-to-day basis. A company's strategy defines what a company does—and will do in the future—and, to some extent, where it will do what it does. How a company will do this is largely tactical and, while extremely important, not truly strategic. Too often in this industry of action, executives jump too quickly to the "how" without first asking "what," or even whether they should undertake an activity in the first place. That is not to say that stopping at "what" is sufficient either; it is simply not part of a company's strategy per se but rather a crucial follow-on step: the tactical action plan, which indeed is highly focused on the "how," along with the "who" and "when." It is essential to follow a strategic planning exercise with the development of a detailed implementation plan that identifies key action steps to effect the strategies and empowers and tasks specific individuals and departments with actionable, concrete steps to pursue and with deadlines and benchmarks for measuring progress.

Vision, Mission, and Values

The starting point of any strategy should be the articulation of a company's vision, mission, and values. These elements define why the company exists, what its purpose is, and what the guiding principles and values of the organization are that define it today and will continue to guide it in the future. These statements should be validated through the strategic planning exercise and tested for relevance at key points during the process. And, in an iterative process, all subsequent elements of the company's strategy should be tested against these statements.

Strategy Pillars

A well-rounded strategy is built on a solid foundation of eight strategy pillars. The strategies available to a real estate company fall into eight distinct categories (figure 1-3). Within each of these categories are individual strategies that every company's management should consider at one time or another.

Figure 1-3: STRATEGY PILLARS

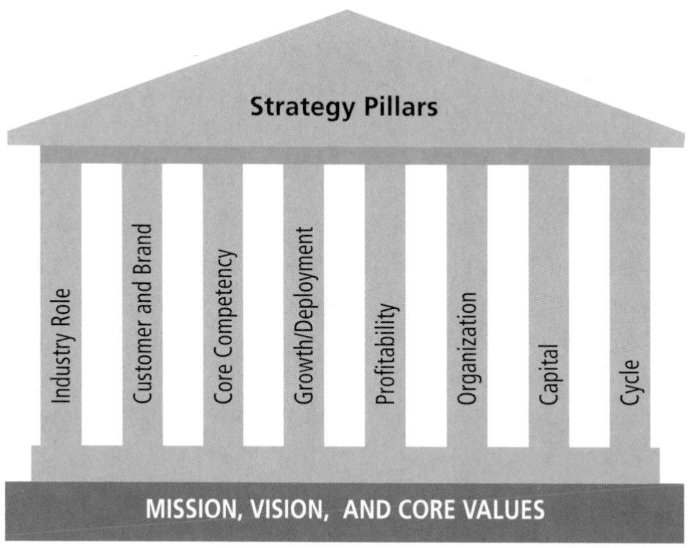

- *Industry Role Strategy.* More than any other factor, this strategy defines the character of the firm. The industry role strategy defines what a company will do and for whom and typically involves defining the company's core business activities, including capital risk and operating risk roles.

- *Customer and Brand Strategy.* This strategy involves identifying who the company's customers or clients are and how they differentiate the company from its competition. While most company leaders have a clear understanding of who their customers or clients are, for others this is an essential part of the strategic planning process. In choosing the customer and brand strategy, the company decides what key promises it makes to its customers, thereby defining its brand.

- *Core Competency Strategy.* This strategy involves identifying and defining what differentiates a company from its competition. Core competencies are what enable the company to do something better, faster, or cheaper than others, thus giving it a competitive advantage in the marketplace. A company that does not have clearly definable core competencies probably is doomed to play a marginal role in the industry and to post mediocre financial results.

- *Growth and Geographic Deployment Strategy.* This set of strategies is related to the growth of the business and where, geographically, it will pursue its chosen industry roles. It focuses on three primary factors: geographic market, product, and customer segment.

- *Profitability Strategy.* This set of strategies is about improving efficiency and increasing the bottom-line profitability of the company. Individual strategies in this category typically are oriented toward ways to reduce the cost of doing business, increase the speed of delivery, and improve both profitability and customer satisfaction.

- *Organizational Strategy.* This set of strategies is focused on how best to organize the business to achieve the company's strategic objectives, pursue its industry roles and geographic deployment strategies, and optimize organizational effectiveness. These strategies define—and, where necessary, modify—the company's organizational structure, with the goal of improving customer, owner, and employee satisfaction as well as the morale of the company and its financial performance.

■ *Capital Strategy.* This set of strategies defines how the company will access and deploy capital. It is formulated purposefully near the end of the strategic planning process so as not to influence decisions regarding industry role, growth, or geographic deployment. A company should first determine what the opportunities are in the marketplace—given the outlook for the economy, the real estate cycle, and the competitive landscape—and then figure out how to fund the opportunity. It is perfectly acceptable to modify the company's appetite or ambition on the basis of a careful examination of capital availability and attendant risk, but it would be a mistake to begin a strategic planning process with the assumption that only so much capital is available.

■ *Cycle Strategy.* Cycle strategies are typically the opposite of growth strategies. They help define, in advance, how a company is going to monitor changes in economic or real estate market cycles and, more important, how it is going to act in the face of changing market conditions. Inertia, rationalization, and denial are powerful natural tendencies that have sunk more than one real estate company over the years. Cycle strategies are intended to inject discipline into the organization's operating practices, so it remains attuned to, anticipates, and is proactive in response to the downturn. They also ensure that the company has the organizational and capital structure first to weather challenging market conditions and then to take advantage of opportunities that inevitably will present themselves in down markets by companies that are not similarly prepared—what Sam Zell referred to as "dancing on other people's graves."

Once the overall strategic direction of the company is completed and approved, it is critical to translate the strategies and goals into a business and implementation plan, which is discussed in more detail in chapter 11. Although not technically strategic, annual business planning is a critical element of the overall planning process. Implementation plans should be designed to track progress as well as assign responsibilities and should set measurable milestones toward achieving strategic goals and objectives.

The eight strategy pillars outlined above complement each other, and multiple strategies in each category should be adopted to reach a company's goals. A company's strategy should be strongly influenced by the current and upcoming phases of the real estate cycle. Therefore, each of the strategies will receive a different emphasis depending on the phase of the cycle (figure 1-4). A company should select the strategy for a given phase as the previous phase ends or the current phase begins. Since the phases of the cycle tend to run two to four years in duration, strategic planning should be conducted at similar or more frequent intervals.

The strategies for the upturn phase typically emphasize capital risk roles and growth strategies. A company should "make hay while the sun shines" and build as much as it reasonably can. Cycle strategies generally are not important during the upturn. Similarly, profitability strategies generally receive little emphasis then, because most of the company's efforts are focused on its capital risk growth strategies. Organizational strategies, however, are paramount as the company gears up for growth; it must both create the organizational capabilities and talent to handle the growth and ensure that the company does not make mistakes. The company should sell assets as the market rises, rather than trying to time the exact top of the cycle, and be prepared to continue selling into the mature phase.

Figure 1-4: STRATEGY EMPHASIS

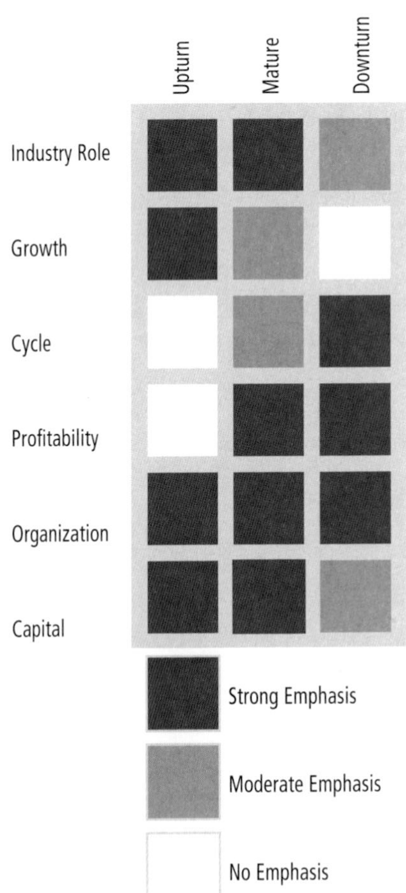

The strategy for the mature phase emphasizes industry role and growth strategies for both capital risk and operating risk businesses, as demand and supply move toward equilibrium and companies seek new or expanded opportunities. Meanwhile, it is essential to make sure that service businesses and the firm's balance sheet are stable and capable of carrying the company through the inevitable downturn. As the company reaches the end of the mature phase, growth strategies become much less important and the company should begin to pursue profitability and capital formation strategies more aggressively in preparation for a possible downturn. Profitability strategies are central to improving profit margins and offsetting the slowdown in growth. Certain cycle strategies may be used in the waning portions of the mature phase, as the company considers shedding unproductive activities. Organizational issues gain prominence as the company settles into a routine that should lead to a more efficient and profitable operation.

The strategy for the downturn focuses on downsizing both capital risk roles and less profitable or "non-core" operations. Cycle strategies become the major focus of the company's strategy in the downturn. Profitability strategies must be emphasized to maintain or increase profitability during this difficult phase. Organizational strategies take on more importance as the company scales down to its essential core activities and, ideally, shifts resources to service businesses. These changes can cause significant pain and dislocation, all of which must be managed.

Subsequent chapters take a more detailed look at each of these strategy pillars. Chapter 11 explores the key elements of a successful strategic planning process. Chapter 12 contains case studies of selected companies that have reached various crossroads and have used strategic planning to chart a path for success.

CHAPTER 2

Mission, Vision, and Core Values

Much has been written over the years on the subject of mission and vision statements and core values. This chapter does not attempt to break new ground, nor is it a guide to help craft the perfect mission statement. It is, however, an acknowledgment that defining a company's mission, vision, and core values are vital elements of any strategic plan.

The development of well-written vision, mission, and values statements signals intent and direction, allowing key stakeholders the opportunity to put their own mark on implementation—an essential part of enthusiastic execution and good governance. In addition, a periodic review of mission and vision compels an organization's leaders to agree on the company's long-term direction and set a new course if one is required to get the organization back on track. Jim Collins and Jerry Porras make a strong case in their book, *Built to Last,*[1] that embracing a vision is part of what distinguishes truly exceptional companies that have withstood the test of time.

Framing an organization's mission, vision, and values takes perseverance, the courage to set one's own stamp on the results, and a desire to live the results rather than tuck them away on a Web site and forget them. All three elements are interconnected and should be discussed and developed together; the strategic planning team must come to a consensus on all of them and be able to communicate them clearly to all the company's employees and stakeholders.

A 2000 survey of more than 1,200 corporate executives indicated that mission and vision statements are among the top five management tools used globally, with 79 percent of all respondents indicating that they had used such statements within the past year.[2] Although many terms have been used to describe these tools (mission, vision, core ideology, core purpose, guiding principles, and so forth), the labels themselves are less important than a company's ability to formulate and communicate these statements, and then define and test individual strategies against these statements for relevance and authenticity. Although it does not really matter how you label the various elements of a company's statement, it important that everyone involved in formulating the strategy is working on the same basic definition before the wordsmithing begins. The feature box below provides some useful definitions.

MISSION STATEMENTS . . .

- Describe an ideal future and are inspirational as well as aspirational.
- Unite an organization in a common, coherent strategic direction.
- Convey a larger sense of organizational purpose, so that employees see themselves as building a cathedral rather than laying stones.
- Answer the question, what impact do we want to have on society?

VISION STATEMENTS . . .

- Support the mission.
- Describe the overall purpose of an organization: what we do, who we do it for, and how and why we do it.
- Set the boundaries of the organization's current activities.
- Are the starting point in developing a strategic direction.

CORE VALUES STATEMENTS . . .

- Reflect the core ideology of an organization, the deeply held values that do not change over time.
- Answer the question, how do we carry out our mission?
- Are the values that the organization lives, breathes, and reflects in all its activities, not the ones you think it should have.

Mission

The mission statement is the starting point of any strategy plan. A mission statement articulates the organization's fundamental reasons for existence and serves as a perpetual guiding star on the horizon. It should be the reason that every employee in the organization gets out of bed in the morning to go to work; it should serve as the epitaph of the company. It goes beyond making money and is not to be confused with specific business goals. To be effective, a mission statement should be a concise assertion of the company's reason for existence, covering what it is, what it does, and how it does it. The mission statement should reflect the company's current direction as well as lay the groundwork for its future. It defines the path the company will take to get to that future. Ideally, it becomes a key communications tool, a way to keep everyone in the company moving in the same direction, in both the short term and the long term. Everyone involved in drafting the mission statement should be aware that completing it is only the beginning of the strategic planning process, not an end in itself. The mission statement should not be filed away and ignored until the next strategic planning process begins; it should be reexamined—and possibly revised—throughout the process and should continue to guide the organization on a daily basis.

As company leaders develop the mission statement, they should focus on keeping it interesting, concise, and to the point. Nobody will remember a dull, bland statement. And a statement that employees cannot remember will not be effective.

A realistic and credible vision focuses on the future but is grounded in the past and present. We have to know where we are and who we are before we can decide where we want to go and how to get there.[3]

Mission Statements

Some particularly good examples of mission statements from the real estate industry and beyond appear in the feature box on the next page.

Although it is perfectly acceptable to revisit and fine-tune a company's mission statement over time, it is probably a bad sign if an organization finds itself compelled to consider a wholesale change in its mission every few years. This can

MISSION STATEMENTS

- AvalonBay Communities: "Enhancing the Lives of Our Residents."
- Apple Computer, Inc., "is committed to bringing the best personal computing experience to students, educators, creative professionals, and consumers around the world through its innovative hardware, software, and Internet offerings."
- The Bozzuto Group "will be the best real estate company in America. We will do this by providing an unparalleled experience for those whose lives we touch. This will be our legacy."
- Classic Residence by Hyatt "is dedicated to providing quality environments, services, and programs to enrich the lives of older adults."
- Fannie Mae: "Our public mission, and our defining goal, is to help more families achieve the American dream of homeownership."
- Google: "To organize the world's information and make it universally accessible and useful."
- Jones Lang LaSalle: "Committed to delivering exceptional strategic, fully integrated services for property owners, investors, and occupiers."
- Southwest Airlines: "Dedication to the highest quality of customer service delivered with a sense of warmth, friendliness, individual pride, and company spirit."
- East West Partners "is a family of related but independent companies devoted to building, selling, managing, and supporting high-quality real estate in the communities in which they operate.

  "We place faith in good people. Each company has broad-based employee ownership with day-to-day management responsibilities. Everyone works to delight customers in every transaction.

  "We are dedicated to innovation. An entrepreneurial spirit is encouraged on the part of each employee, thus helping avoid 'commodity' products or services that have little added value for our customers.

  "We recognize that we all have responsibilities. We understand that it is 'good business' to give back to the communities in which we work, and to vigorously protect the natural environment."

indicate that a company has lost its rudder or perhaps has not done a particularly effective job of defining itself.

Interestingly, Bozzuto, Southwest, and Forrest City all have mission statements that also outline their visions. They state a purpose and the methods of delivering on that purpose.

Strategic Vision

A company's vision supports the organization's mission statement. It describes what the company is going to do or how it is going to realize the mission for the strategy planning horizon. It provides the governing criteria for the creation and evaluation of strategic initiatives. The strategic vision statement further articulates who the company is, what it does, and how it does it under the umbrella of the company mission.

Unlike a mission statement, which should not radically change from one phase of the real estate cycle to the next, it is reasonable to assume that a real estate company's strategic vision for how it is going to execute its mission will change and adjust over time. The stated mission of Champion Development Group—a Los Angeles–based developer of mixed-use projects—is "to be the best urban infill developer in California by developing or renovating award-winning projects in A+ locations; to deliver trend-setting and innovative designs with superior financial returns; to gain recognition as significant contributors to environment and community; and to create customers who believe our projects are the best place to live, shop, dine, or work." Champion has revised its strategic vision as its business has grown and evolved. Its new strategy is to expand what it does—to building, buying, and financing projects—and to expand the geographic area in which it operates—to the entire western United States.

Articulating the vision statement is a creative process, according to Collins and Porras. Envisioning involves the creation of a potential future rather than prediction. The envisioned future involves such essential questions as "Does it get our juices flowing? Do we find it stimulating? Does it spur forward momentum? The envisioned future should be so exciting in its own right that it would continue to keep the organization motivated even if the leaders who set the goal disappeared."[4]

Whereas a company's mission statement typically is a public statement of its core purpose and raison d'être—and is often leveraged to describe a company in marketing materials, signage, advertisements, and elsewhere—the vision statement is more often developed primarily for internal use, to serve as a framework for strategic planning and for making other decisions. It is important not to confuse a mission or vision statement with an advertising or marketing slogan, which can change frequently, based on short-term needs and trends in the marketplace (see box below).

AN EXAMPLE: FORD MOTOR COMPANY

Our Vision

- To become the world's leading consumer company for automotive products and services.

Our Mission

- We are a global family with a proud heritage passionately committed to providing personal mobility for people around the world.
- We anticipate consumer need and deliver outstanding products and services that improve people's lives.

Ford's statements are a good example of how labels, mission, vision, and so forth are less important than what the statements convey. Their vision statement (we would call this a mission statement) is inspirational: "to become the world's leading consumer company" for cars. How are they going to achieve this mission? By providing "personal mobility for people." They will do so by anticipating what they want and delivering great quality. Where? Globally. Now, you can argue whether Ford has been successful in achieving its objectives of late, but it is hard to say that there is any lack of clarity with respect to the company's vision and mission.

Core Values

Core values, often referred to as guiding principles, are essential and enduring tenets that are not to be compromised for financial gain or short-term expediency. A company's core values should not change over time. It may be appropriate to revise the language and bring greater clarity to the statements for example, but a company should not treat its employees and customers with respect one day, then drop this attitude as a core value the next. Core values help define what a company is and what it stands for; they are the principles by which a company navigates and the glue that holds it together. Collins and Porras point out that "Companies that enjoy enduring success have core values and a core purpose that remain fixed while their business strategies and practices endlessly adapt to a changing world. . . . Truly great companies understand the difference between what should never change and what should be open for change."[5]

Collins and Porras advise executives to be relentlessly honest when identifying their company's core values, to ask themselves "What core values do we truly and passionately hold?"[6] They urge corporate leaders to articulate which values are central to the organization, those that will stand the test of time. "The point," they note, "is that a great company decides for itself what values it holds to be core, largely independent of the current environment, competitive requirements, or management fads."[7] They also comment that successful companies tend to have only a few core values—usually between three and five—because only a few values can be so fundamental and so deeply held that they can truly be defined as core.

Integrity, teamwork, creativity, communication, innovation, quality, diversity, respect, responsibility, professionalism, hard work, passion, environmental stewardship, and a customer focus often are listed as corporate core values. Company leaders should discuss and articulate precisely what these words and phrases mean to the organization before including them in their list of core values. They should not include something just because it sounds good (or makes the company sound good); rather, they must ensure that each stated core value truly reflects their organization.

Most important, company leaders should not confuse core values with core competencies (discussed in detail in chapter 5). Core competencies define the organization's capabilities—what it is good at—whereas core values define the company culture—what it stands for and how its employees are expected to conduct themselves in their business dealings.

Some particularly good examples of core values and guiding principles from the real estate industry appear in the feature box on the following page.

Taken together, mission, strategic vision, and core value statements should stretch—but not stress—the organization's capabilities and give shape and direction to its future. They should provide a framework within which the company's culture, values, and initiatives can evolve over the long term (at least five to seven years, and possibly much longer). Although the statements can be as short as several words or as long as a few pages, shorter statements tend to be more memorable and therefore have a meaningful impact on a company's strategy.

CORE VALUES

The Bozzuto Group

- Concern for the people and communities we touch.
- Creativity in everything we do.
- Aggressiveness in the pursuit of customer satisfaction and business growth.
- Perfection: a value worth pursuing; one that through our efforts we hope to achieve.

Trammell Crow Company

Uses the acronym RISE for its corporate values, stating, "Our corporate values are the foundation upon which our company is built.

- Respect: Treat everyone with dignity, value their contributions, and help one another succeed.
- Integrity: Uphold the highest standards in our business practices.
- Service: Dedicate ourselves to making a meaningful impact with our clients and in our communities.
- Excellence: Aspire to be the best in everything we do and drive for continuous improvement."

Trico Homes of Calgary

Uses acronym TRICO to convey its guiding principles, and as a result, most employees can recite the values:

- Trust,
- Respect,
- Integrity,
- Community, and
- Opportunity.

Endnotes

[1] Collins, James C., and Jerry I. Porras, *Built to Last: Successful Habits of Visionary Companies* (New York: Collins, 2004).

[2] Rigby, Darrell, and Barbara Bilodeau, *Management Tools and Trends 2007* (Boston: Bain & Company, 2007).

[3] Kozlow, David, "A Perspective on Strategic Planning: What's Your Vision?" *Economic Development Review,* 16 (2): 5–9.

[4] Collins, James C., and Jerry I. Porras, "Building Your Company's Vision," *Harvard Business Review,* September–October 1996, 65–77.

[5] Collins and Porras, "Building Your Company's Vision," pp. 65–66.

[6] Ibid, p. 71.

[7] Ibid, p. 67.

CHAPTER 3

Industry Role Strategy

Perhaps the most important strategic decision made by top management is which industry role or roles a company should play. Industry roles are all about what a company does, and to some extent for whom—principally whether for the company's own account or for others—and have a strong intersection with where the company operates. More than any other factor, industry roles—whether they are the capital risk roles or the operating risk service businesses shown in figure 3-1—define the character of the company.

Decisions about industry role should be based on the opportunities available in the marketplace, the strengths and weaknesses of the organization, and the preferences of top management. Simply put, an industry role strategy should respond to two questions: What is the company not doing today that it should be doing, given market opportunities, the particular strengths and weaknesses of the organization, possible synergies, and the potential to make money doing them? And what is the company doing today that it should not be doing, possibly because another company can do these things better, faster, or cheaper? A company should consider outsourcing those roles that it has not identified as critical core competencies, but that it wishes to have available in the arsenal to execute its overall strategy. Many companies reach the point of inertia and continue in their traditional roles simply because "we've always done it." It is important to challenge that inertia.

Figure 3-1: REAL ESTATE INDUSTRY ROLES

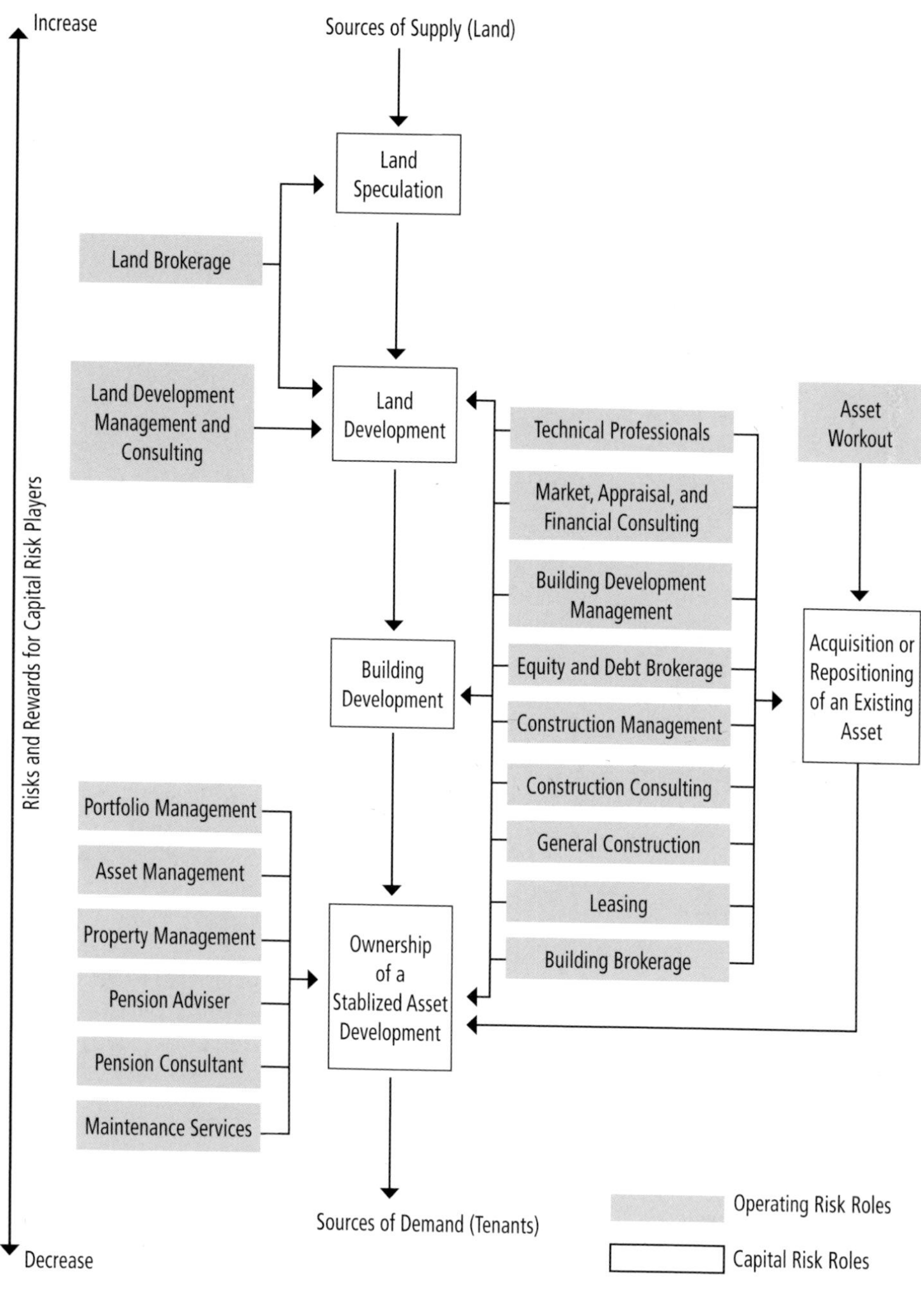

With realistic information about the strengths and weaknesses of the company and its competition, top management can eliminate some of the potential industry roles that would undermine the organization's success. As the firm moves into a new role or attempts to shore up an existing one, information on company strengths and weaknesses helps highlight those skills that must be developed among staff members and indicates the type of talent that must be recruited.

The John Frank Company is an example of a company that got into serious trouble while building its first luxury high-rise condominium project—Millennium Tower—because it did not have any experience building high-rise buildings. The company was extremely competent at developing low-rise and mid-rise rental apartments and condominiums, but it did not acquire—or outsource—the expertise necessary to develop a luxury high-rise project successfully, and thus suffered the consequences. John Frank, the company's founder and CEO, admitted that he fell in love with the project, which made it difficult for him to be objective about critical design and value engineering decisions, at least initially, that were necessary to turn the project around. Companies that are not careful about picking their industry role or that attempt to move into new markets or types of development without first acquiring—or outsourcing—the skills needed to succeed at such ventures must be prepared to pay "the dumb tax."

Another important component of the decision about industry role is understanding what roles the market demands. Companies that define themselves solely as developers when the market does not need developers eventually will go out of business, if they do not have a strong balance sheet.

In addition, it is important to recognize that the market demands different roles during different phases of the real estate cycle. Development services, for example, are in demand during an upturn and workout services during a downturn. Likewise, the real estate cycle may have a significant impact on the returns provided to certain roles, particularly those of land speculation and development.

It also is important for company leaders to think about the industry roles that a company could or should play in a context that is independent of the company's current corporate and capital structure and its core competencies and capabilities, at least initially. The strategic planning process should explore all possible industry roles; it should be based on a fairly dispassionate view of the attendant risks and returns, the opportunities, and the competitive landscape. Although decision makers might eventually circle back and decide that it does not make sense to take on a particular role—based on the effort involved in learning how to undertake that new activity or the company's ability to finance it—it is still worthwhile to consider all possibilities in the early stages of the strategic planning process.

As part of the strategic planning process, it is almost as important to decide what roles a company is not going to play as to decide what roles it will play. Doing so will avoid confusion and wasted energy and will provide everyone in the organization with a clear strategic roadmap to guide their activities.

After determining the organization's strengths and weaknesses, marketplace opportunities, and top management's preferences, it is important to understand what each potential business or service line (industry role) demands of a real estate firm. Each role and service business carries entirely different types of risk and requires specialized skills and core competencies.

As discussed earlier, there are two basic types of industry roles: (a) capital risk roles, which involve investing equity capital for real estate development or acquisition, and (b) operating risk roles, which are fee income activities that put only minimal amounts of working capital at risk.

Strategic Balance

The major question facing companies that predominantly play capital risk roles in the real estate industry—primarily land speculators, land developers, building developers, and those that acquire or reposition existing buildings—is how to weather the downturn phase that is an inevitable part of the real estate cycle.

Companies that play capital risk roles face two options. The first is to develop sufficient cash flow from owned assets and cash or cash equivalents to maintain the organization in every phase of the real estate cycle, especially during downturns. This is the ideal structure for such firms, and usually results from the conservative funding of such capital risk activities as building development. One example of a company with a steady, cash-flowing business that uses its "excess" capital to take big risks in development projects is the H.G. Fenton Company, which uses the modified debt-coverage ratio from its owned portfolio to cover current income needs while funneling excess revenues into development deals. Similarly, a family trust requires the Crosland Group to produce a certain amount of income, and the company reinvests excess income in its development projects.

Unfortunately, few capital risk players have sufficient unleveraged assets to take this approach. Therefore, most such players must pursue the second option for survival during periodic downturns: adding operating risk service businesses to balance their corporate portfolios. Just as personal financial advisers stress the need for an investment portfolio that is balanced between high-risk growth stocks and low-risk utilities or government bonds, the high-risk capital roles of the real estate industry may be balanced by lower-risk operating businesses. To survive downturns, most companies have little choice but to rely on operating service businesses. Transwestern Property Company did this so well during the Texas real estate depression of the late 1980s—becoming, as Transwestern Management Company, one of the largest asset management companies in the United States—that its development business did not keep up with its new core business. When the markets shifted to warrant new development, Transwestern had to invest heavily and mount a new initiative to rebuild the infrastructure required to compete in development. (See chapter 12, page 187, for more details.)

Another example: East West Partners is a family of related but independent companies that build, sell, manage, and support real estate projects. Its service companies help keep its capital risk companies afloat during downturns. And LCOR began providing third-party advisory and consulting services as well as fee development services for the federal government and other entities during the downturn of the early 1990s before returning to the development of speculative, at-risk development projects for its own account in the late 1990s. The lesson here is that when the development opportunities "cylinder" of the real estate engine is not firing, the company that has a property management entity or other operating risk service business, or a portfolio of income-producing properties, is better able to survive periods of inactivity on the capital risk side.

Many capital risk players view service businesses as no more than a port in a storm to be abandoned once the next upturn begins. To be effective, however, service businesses must be supported and expanded continuously. They cannot be turned on and off without losing the goodwill and value of the franchise, which may take years to rebuild. In addition, abandoning service businesses in an upturn and returning to them in a downturn means rebuilding the organization—reinventing the wheel—every four or five years. Finally, viable service businesses expose the company to the many capital risk opportunities that never reach the open market.

In summary, most contemporary real estate companies are as solidly built as a four-legged stool, with development activities that generate development fee income; management activities that generate acquisition, disposition, and ongoing management fee income; ownership activities that generate ongoing income from properties held for long-term cash flow and appreciation; and capital gains activities that generate income by recapitalizing or selling owned properties at the appropriate time (figure 3-2).

Figure 3-2: STRATEGIC BALANCE

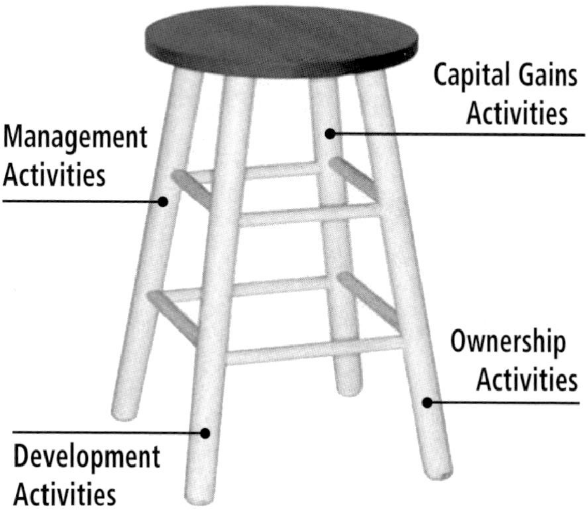

Capital Risk Roles

The various capital risk roles involve distinct activities that add value to the development and ownership of real estate, from site acquisition to entitlement, to horizontal land development, to vertical building development, and so forth (figure 3-3).

With the end of each role, a company can decide either to sell the property to another capital risk player, who will assume the next role, or simply to take responsibility for the next role itself. If the firm that originated the project decides to assume the next role, it must recognize that it effectively has made the decision to purchase the evolving asset at the then-market price.

It is not all that unusual to learn that many real estate companies do not know which of their industry roles make money. The reason is that they either transfer their assets internally at cost rather than at market price or use inaccurate cost

Figure 3-3 : CAPITAL RISK ROLES

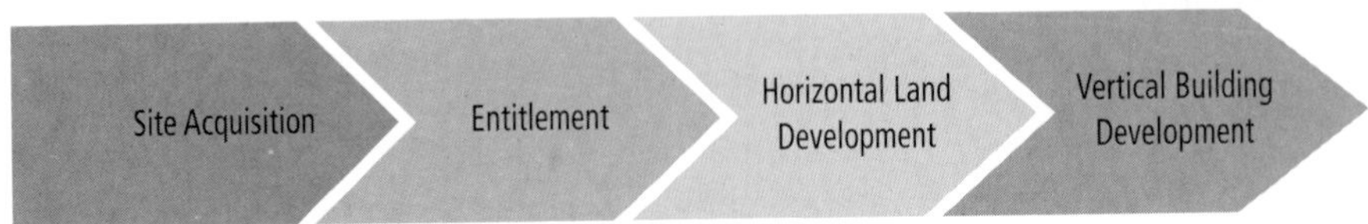

allocations and are not disciplined about marking to market, thereby underestimating the risk and profit to be made by choosing to undertake certain roles.

Many capital risk land and building developers assume that they make their money on the last step in the process: the sale of a built and stabilized project. In many instances, however, the building development role merely pulls the improved land through the pipeline, with most of the profit earned from the land development activities. Sometimes the company can make as much risk-adjusted profit—if not more—by selling the improved land to another building developer. Although management and staff forgo the satisfaction of seeing the building completed, the company significantly reduces its financial risk and stress and frees its capital and human resources for new investments.

For example, during the last for-sale housing boom, many developers of rental apartment projects could not get projects to pencil out. The demand for rentals was lagging because of historically low interest rates and flight to ownership, and the amount of money that condo developers and investors were willing to pay for land meant that many apartment projects just did not make sense. Some rental developers decided to jump into the for-sale market, while others decided to sell land in inventory that was "overpriced" as rentals to other condo developers and homebuilders. Instead of adding for-sale vertical development to their mix of industry roles, a number of companies decided to sell the land they were holding to the highest bidder. According to a regional partner of a national apartment developer/operator, the division made more money in the past cycle simply by selling land than it ever had through vertical construction of apartments. They did the math, analyzed the alternatives, and discovered that they would make a larger profit by selling the land at the peak of the condominium cycle than they would have if they were to build and sell apartments or take on the additional risk of building condominiums themselves.

The major capital risk industry roles are discussed in the following sections.

Land Speculation

Land speculators purchase or gain control of land with the aim of profiting from anticipated price appreciation, typically with no intention of entitling, improving the land, or ever engaging in development activities. They earn a profit by tying up land at a favorable price, holding it, and selling it in a future seller's market; by increasing the land's value by making off-site infrastructure improvements; by creating a higher and better land use for a changing market; by realizing appreciation from changing metropolitan area growth trends; or by some combination of these four methods.

Risk. Land speculation carries the highest risk because of the investment's lack of liquidity, the potential need for significant patient equity, political as well as market uncertainties, and the limited possibility of cash flow. In addition, land value is typically the most volatile component in the industry. Builders tend to buy land heavily during the upswing of the cycle, especially when they fall behind in their ability to produce lots and homes when the market is particularly hot. When the market slows down, they often find themselves with excess—and often devalued—inventory. Builders typically prefer to have two to three years' worth of lot inventory on their books. When the market slows down, what seemed like two to three years of inventory during a peak absorption period suddenly becomes five or more years of inventory. Builders then stop buying new land and try to sell their excess land, in an environment in which few or no other builders are willing to buy it. Thus begin the price cuts—something that happened throughout the United States in 2007, after the 2005 housing market downturn. Land was selling at very deep discounts from its peak prices, with very few buyers.

Return. Land speculation can yield the highest return when land is purchased at a favorable price during a downturn. Indeed, staggering returns are possible, depending on the use of the land and the value created by that use. During a downturn, of course, raw land values may be "under water," meaning that the residual land value is negative as a result of holding costs such as real estate taxes, debt service, and the lack of short-term demand. A builder in the mid-Atlantic recently purchased some land but then got into trouble and was unable to build on it. When he tried to sell it back to the land developer at 50 cents on the dollar, he met with no success; the landowner, flush with excess inventory himself, figured he would wait to buy it back from the bank at some point in the future for 10 cents on the dollar. Land values can drop very quickly, and speculators who are too heavily invested in land can find themselves in a difficult position. In some case, profits usually are possible only in the upturn and mature phases of the real estate cycle; both the highest risks and the highest returns come toward the end of the mature phase.

Core Competencies. Land speculation requires excellent relationships with land brokers or contacts with landowners. It also demands an understanding of development trends in the metropolitan area where the land speculator operates. Land speculators need to have access to significant patient capital that does not require short-term return, and they can support only a low amount of overhead.

Horizontal Land Development

The horizontal land development role involves the transformation of raw land—through political entitlements and physical improvements—into a site that is ready for building construction. In addition to on-site improvements such as internal roads, the utility system, and lot grading, physical improvements also may include off-site improvements such as roads and utilities that serve the property.

Risk. Land development is nearly as risky as land speculation, because of the investment's illiquidity, the low level of leverage typically available compared with the level available for vertical construction, political as well as market uncertainties, and the possibility of no cash flow.

Return. The potential returns in land development are almost as high as those of land speculation, particularly if the land is located in a market with a high barrier to entry (such as a community with strict growth controls) and the developer is skilled in obtaining the entitlements or zoning changes that permit a higher and better use, increased density, and the like. However, these returns can be significantly affected by the real estate cycle.

Core Competencies. Land development requires political skills—including the ability to obtain entitlements or zoning changes—as well as strong project management and oversight skills. Land developers must have access to patient capital that does not require short-term returns during the entitlement and holding periods, as well as access to significant capital for the infrastructure construction and marketing stages. Land developers must operate with a relatively low amount of overhead during the planning and entitlement stages, and then must know how to gear up for the labor-intensive infrastructure construction stage.

Vertical Building Development

The building development role calls for the vertical construction of one or more buildings (or homes) on improved land with the intent of generating cash flow by leasing or selling the structure(s). In the case of an income-producing asset, the building's value is determined by the cash flow it generates and how the market values that cash flow, regardless of land and construction costs.

Risk. Initial risk may be high, first because of potential construction risk—construction cost overruns that could require additional equity infusion, which may result in reduced ownership by the developer—and, later, because of marketing risk—if the building is leased or sold, or in competition that is too intense, resulting in lower revenue because of low lease rates or sale prices or slow lease-up or sale. Assuming realistic knowledge of the market without unjustified developer optimism, however, the risk of this role is moderate. The risk can be extremely low if a significant portion of a project is preleased or presold. In fact, the risk can be reduced to just the on-time and on-budget completion of construction, which, in turn, can be bonded if the project is completely preleased or presold.

Return. Returns from building development, although potentially very high, are moderate in comparison with those that can be achieved through land speculation and land development. Returns can be significantly affected by the state of the local economy and the amount and timing of the competition during the lease-up or sale period. Many times, the return on building development is negligible, although the building development role may pull the improved land value through the pipeline and yield a land development profit faster than a sale to a third party. Developers can boost their returns by contributing or deferring development fees as equity participation for a share of the profits or returns off the back end of the deal, typically in increasing amounts after certain investment hurdles are achieved.

Core Competencies. Comprehensive building development skills—in permitting, construction, financing and capital formation, planning and design, and customer and marketing strategy—are required to handle this complicated and diverse role. Building developers also must have a sophisticated understanding of individual metropolitan area markets and market segment trends and have strong project management and oversight skills. This role also requires strong capital market skills, including the ability to tap both debt and equity sources.

Acquisition or Repositioning of an Existing Asset

The role associated with the acquisition and repositioning of an existing asset involves the purchase of a building for market repositioning through better leasing and management, renovation, or conversion to a completely different use or adaptive use.

Risk. Assuming realistic knowledge of the market and no irrational exuberance, the risk is moderate, since the asset is already built and has an operating history. This risk is lower than the level of risk associated with new building development, but it could increase if significant marketing repositioning or renovation is required. In some instances, the risk can be slightly greater than that associated with new building development, because the construction risks of renovation tend to be higher and can be more difficult to bond. An existing structure often yields surprises behind the walls.

Return. The potential returns can be quite attractive, particularly where the building, after accounting for the improvement and repositioning costs, can be acquired below replacement cost, which is a possibility if the property is in foreclosure or the seller needs to dispose of it quickly during a downturn.

Core Competencies. As with vertical building development, this complicated and diverse role demands experienced building development talent, as well as a sophisticated understanding of trends in individual metropolitan area markets and market segments, strong project management skills, and the ability to manage the capital markets.

Ownership of a Stabilized Asset

Ownership of a stabilized asset involves the purchase of an existing building whose cash flow is reasonably predictable. The purchaser generally is an institution, a real estate company looking for a foundation to its business, a REIT, a wealthy individual, a private partnership or private equity fund, a corporation, or another investor attempting to minimize risk while investing in real estate.

Risk. The risk associated with owning a stabilized asset generally is low, particularly if a commercial building is occupied by credit tenants. (The level of risk rises to moderate if noncredit tenants are involved.) In addition, if asset owners do not maintain or improve their competitive position in the market, they may discover that their asset has grown obsolete or needs to be repositioned. Rental apartments tend to be among the least risky income-producing asset classes: although cash flows can be affected by downturns, most households need a place to live and apartment owners have the ability to influence occupancies by adjusting rents.

Return. Owners can expect moderate returns—typically in the range of 6 to 12 percent—and a predictable cash flow, particularly if the tenants are creditworthy. Historically, cash-on-cash returns have varied greatly, mostly as a function of the quantity of capital that is chasing real estate, the performance of other investment alternatives, and the rate of inflation. Owners of stabilized assets have the ability to pull tax-free money out of the asset through refinancing, are able to benefit from depreciation, and regularly engage in tax-free exchanges of assets to restart the depreciation clock and rebalance portfolios.

Core Competencies. Ownership of a stabilized asset requires experience and talent in asset management and marketing as well as an understanding of market and submarket trends. Substantial initial equity with a relatively high degree of patience is also needed.

Operating Risk Roles

The universe of real estate service businesses shares a common characteristic of generally carrying only operating risk—that is, the service fee alone is at risk—and relatively modest overhead capital risk. Besides their lower level of risk, nearly all operating risk businesses have a similar financial structure. Working capital equal to 12 to 20 percent of the business's annual revenues is permanently invested in the company. This capital primarily funds the company's accounts receivable, although it also might amortize startup costs.

Service business profitability typically ranges from 10 to 20 percent of revenues, although some firms have achieved margins as high as 40 percent. Thus, a company can usually fund its growth from internal sources simply by keeping some or all the profits in the business as working capital. The major exception to this financial structure is general contracting, which must tie up significant equity to obtain the bonding capacity sufficient to bid on larger contracts.

The various operating risk roles available to the real estate industry are outlined in the following sections. As noted, several of these roles also may involve capital risk.

Land Brokerage

Land brokers facilitate the sale and purchase of tracts of land. They typically represent landowners and bring together the buyer and seller in a land sales transaction. They also work with buyers who are seeking properties for specific land uses. As a seller's agent, brokers try to maximize the value of the property they represent.

Risk. Land brokerage is a strictly commission-based business, and as such, the risk associated with this operating role is typically very low—usually limited to working capital that is tied up in office leases, equipment, draws against commissions, and the like.

Return. Individual brokers can receive handsome compensation in the upturn and mature phases of the real estate cycle. The return to the business is typically only moderate, but it can be attractive in relationship to the capital required to operate.

Core Competencies. Land brokers must have up-to-date knowledge of local land areas and an understanding of the competitive market, existing owners and their motivations, and the potential land uses surrounding a specific property.

Land Development Management

Land development managers facilitate the land development process for the landowner. Their responsibilities may include overseeing the planning and entitlement of land, managing capital for development projects, improving raw land—clearing and grading, installing roads and utility services, securing political entitlements, and so forth—to the point that the land is suitably prepared to accommodate building construction, and marketing and selling the approved, if not improved, land.

Risk. Although this role may lead to more active involvement in a project, including a capital risk role, development managers generally act as capital risk developers without taking on the associated risk.

Return. Returns for this role can vary depending upon the amount of participation that a land development manager can negotiate. Compensation for these services typically is in the form of a fixed fee—usually a monthly retainer—and possibly a back-end kicker tied to performance or profitability.

Core Competencies. Effective land development managers typically have a proven track record as capital risk developers. In addition to their construction management and marketing skills, they need outstanding communication skills and must be able to shepherd projects through local jurisdictions' often complex entitlement and approval processes. They generally deal directly with various municipal agencies and neighborhood groups, which have a much greater voice in how developers design and build projects today than they have had in the past.

Technical Professionals and Consultants

Technical professionals provide legal, architectural, land planning, engineering, traffic management, parking, environmental, and other services. Market, appraisal, and financial consultants provide project analysis, including market overviews, financial feasibility studies, and marketing strategy advice, to capital risk players involved in land development, building development, acquisitions, and ownership of a stabilized asset. As part of these services, consultants determine the highest and best use(s), optimum type and mix of uses, market opportunities, competitive positioning, product programming, market depth, potential absorption, cash flow projections, merchandising, leasing terms, and advertising required to market a project. An appraisal can determine the value of an asset either in its current condition or upon improvement.

Risk. The risk profile of these roles is low, typically limited to working capital and overhead.

Return. Typically, technical professionals conduct their work on a fixed-fee for service basis. Returns are typically low to moderate compared with capital risk roles, but they can be very attractive considering the low level of capital commitment that is required.

Core Competencies. These roles require in-depth technical expertise and experience in the particular area of specialization, as well as access to—and the ability to analyze—up-to-date market, financial, and other data.

Building Development Management

Like the land development manager, the building development manager provides development services similar to those conducted by a developer, but for a fee.

Risk. Unlike capital risk roles such as building development and build to suit, building development management involves no assumption of capital risk.

Return. While the risk profile may be low, returns can often be increased through participation in the project returns. Upon successful completion of a project, the building owner often pays the building development manager a back-end kicker or bonus based on successful completion, in addition to the base compensation.

Core Competencies. Building development managers must have all the skills of a capital risk building developer.

Equity Brokerage

Investment bankers, syndicators, and bankers can take on the role of raising equity for capital risk players at the project or corporate level. Equity brokers find equity sources and usually provide investment analysis and equity financing sources for both existing and proposed properties. Equity can be raised either privately or publicly and will require investment analysis, deal structuring, identification of capital sources, and transaction closing skills. Parties involved in equity formation often also provide debt formation services; the line separating equity formation and debt brokerage has become blurred as more firms provide both services.

Risk. This role may involve a moderate level of risk, since a firm may expend significant amounts of time with no guarantee that it will be able to raise the money and thus earn its fee.

Return. Compensation generally is based on a percentage of the money raised or on a fee, although some reward for project performance also may be paid.

Core Competencies. The equity formation role requires financial sophistication and the ability to access multiple sources of capital that often have changing requirements and interest levels.

Debt Brokerage

Debt brokers secure debt for capital risk players at the project or corporate level. They usually are hired to identify mezzanine and conventional debt sources, and thus bring together the debt source and the capital risk player. Mortgage bankers and brokers place the funds of insurance companies, conduits, or other institutional investors into specific projects. Bank affiliates, known as conduits and structured investment vehicles, collect and bundle loans to create diverse pools, which then are separated into units by the risk characteristics of each loan and sold in the public markets. Conduits may originate themselves or use the investment of others. Commercial bankers also raise private pools (or syndications) for very large single asset or corporate financing vehicles. As mentioned above, the line separating equity and debt brokerage has become blurred as more firms provide both services.

Risk. Conduits face a moderate level of risk when the market is stable, because of the warehousing component of their business. The risk may be substantially higher when volatility is introduced into the market, as it is today with backups and rising interest rates.

Return. Compensation is based on a percent age of the money raised or on a fee. The percentage is typically low, and the key to success, therefore, is attaining a sufficiently high volume.

Core Competencies. Like the equity brokerage role, the debt brokerage role also requires financial sophistication and the ability to access multiple sources of capital that often have changing requirements and interest levels.

Construction Management

The construction manager is the owner's representative during the construction or renovation process. The manager coordinates and facilitates the on-time, on-budget construction and acts as the liaison between the development team and the general contractor. In the liaison role, the construction manager is responsible for evaluating the effects of design changes on construction timing and project cost, and incorporating these changes into the overall schedule and budget. To minimize project time and cost while maintaining quality, function, and aesthetics, the construction manager generally oversees the contracts of the general contractor during the project's bidding, award, and construction phases.

Construction consultants provide construction managers with advice related to cost estimates for building, detailed cash flow analysis, and construction scheduling. Consultants determine the equipment and manpower needed to complete construction, anticipate timing until project completion, prepare cost estimates, and provide support to the construction manager, who supervises the construction process. Consultants are brought in at the beginning of and during the construction process.

Risk. The risk profile of these operating roles is fairly low, as managers and consultants do not have the completion guarantee risk of a developer or general contractor.

Return. Fees are typically modest and are typically structured on a time and expense basis or as a percentage of the construction cost.

Core Competencies. Effective construction management and consulting requires state-of-the-art knowledge of all aspects of the construction process, insight into the many ways contractors can increase costs, and the ability to stay on top of a demanding schedule.

General Construction

General contracting services are used for land development, shell construction, and tenant improvement work. The general contractor builds a specific project for a capital risk player within a defined time frame based on the plans and specifications developed by the architect and engineer. The general contractor may negotiate for a job or win a contract through a competitive bid based on a set of architectural drawings and project specifications. There are two basic types of contracts. In a fixed-price contract—typically used when all plans and specifications are complete—the general contractor agrees to complete the job for a fixed price, as long as the plans and specs do not change. General construction jobs more commonly are carried out on a cost-plus basis, with the general contractor marking up the actual costs by a negotiated percentage to cover overhead and profit. Cost-plus contracts are appropriate when the probable costs, such as those involved in the rehabilitation of a historic structure, are difficult to forecast. The most common contract today—the cost-plus-fixed-fee contract—is essentially a cost-plus contract with a guaranteed maximum fee. With this type of contract, the contractor and the developer share any savings.

Risk. The risks are moderate but their impact can be painful if challenging cost overruns, guarantees, and bonding are encountered.

Return. Because general contractors work on very small margins, their returns also are moderate.

Core Competencies. General contractors must have in-depth construction knowledge and the ability to work effectively with subcontractors. They also generally must have the capacity to be bonded.

Leasing

The leasing agent is either a tenant or owner representative who facilitates the leasing of office, retail, business park, industrial, or rental apartment space. The leasing agent formulates and executes the leasing process. In the case of building development or repositioning of an existing asset, leasing usually begins well before construction is complete. Working within the constraints of all applicable laws and regulations, leasing agents respond to and balance the often opposing needs of the tenants and the owner (the capital risk player).

The landlord leasing function comprises many elements, including canvassing tenants, showing space and providing relevant materials to prospective tenants, helping to set lease rates and terms, specifying who bears the various operating costs, identifying the special needs of the user, and planning space. Tenant representation, a relatively new specialty service, provides advice to users—particularly corporations—on finding new space and negotiating favorable leases.

Risk. Risks are low and typically limited to working capital.

Return. Here too, successful leasing professionals can be highly compensated, but the returns to the business are moderate.

Core Competencies. Leasing agents must have access to a sophisticated, up-to-date market database and be part of a network of leasing brokers throughout the market, whether they are officially affiliated or not.

Building Brokerage

The building broker may represent both buyers and sellers in the acquisition or sale of an existing property. As part of this commission-based service, the building broker tries to determine the value of the building based on rent performance, type of tenant profile, building location, comparable sales, and capitalization rates. Residential brokers represent buyers and sellers in home purchases. Some companies specialize in sales and marketing of new construction, while others concentrate on the resale of existing properties.

Risk. Risks are low and typically limited to working capital.

Return. Again, individual brokers can make hefty commissions, but the returns to the business are moderate.

Core Competencies. Brokers must have up-to-date knowledge of local building owners and potential buyers.

Asset Workout

Asset workout consultants identify the market and financial problems that plague an owner's assets and prepare a workout plan for resolving those problems. Typically, a property owner retains an asset workout specialist after a specific property runs into financial difficulties, such as insufficient cash flow to cover debt service. Successful workouts do more than merely help a property owner decide whether to retain or sell an asset. They provide an understanding of all of the property's operational aspects, so that the owner can take practical steps to resolve the identified problems within current market conditions.

Risk. Typically the risk profile for asset workout specialists is very low, with the principal risk being working capital and modest amounts of overhead.

Return. Returns are also modest, with most work conducted on a fee-for-services basis. However, some asset workout specialists are able negotiate a back-end kicker or transaction fee if a project performs particularly well.

Core Competencies. Workout specialists must have established, credible relationships with financial institutions, which tend to hold failed projects that have reverted to them, as well as development restructuring and marketing skills.

Asset Management

Asset management is a different business than property management, although many in the real estate industry often confuse the two or blur the line. At its core, asset management is all about understanding and making decisions about the investment life cycle of an asset or a portfolio of properties and is aimed at determining when to sell, renovate, reposition, or recapitalize assets. The asset manager also oversees and evaluates the property manager. Property management, at its core, is about making sure that a building is properly maintained and well occupied.

Asset managers take responsibility for advising on a capital risk owner's real estate portfolio, particularly its long-term value and ongoing bottom-line performance. In this capacity, asset managers may be charged with retaining and supervising the activities of consultants, brokers, and management firms to investigate, analyze, or implement the repositioning or selling of assets or classes of assets and overseeing the property managers for each of the capital risk owner's properties. At the same time, asset managers focus on the capital risk owner's entire real estate portfolio in an effort to obtain the highest possible return on long-term real estate investments.

Asset management often includes asset repositioning, such as the renovation of a building to ensure its competitiveness, lease analysis, re-leasing, and other important issues that may arise in a tenant-driven asset class. Most building developers who maintain an ongoing ownership interest in a stabilized asset also are asset managers, whether they recognize it or not (and whether they charge for it or not).

Risk. The risk profile of this role is low, typically limited to working capital and modest amounts of overhead.

Return. Annual asset management fees typically range from 0.5 to 1.25 percent of the asset value, although this can vary significantly with the size of the asset or portfolio.

Core Competencies. Asset managers typically need most of the skills required of a building developer, particularly if the asset must be significantly repositioned. If they provide additional services, such as property management, leasing, and so forth, they also must be able to manage the inherent conflict of interest—the tension between recommending a sale of an asset and the desire to continue to collect management fees.

Property Management

Property managers take responsibility for the day-to-day operations of a building, including maintenance and operation, marketing and leasing, tenant relations and retention, preparation of the operating budget, rent collection, accounting, reporting to the asset manager or owner, and so forth.

Many development companies manage their own properties, and some provide third-party fee management services for others. They believe this is critical to their success and is an integral part of their investment "story." Many private sector investment builders of apartments, such as Trammell Crow Residential (TCR), JPI, and others, also have maintained a core property management industry role, arguing that while it may not be profitable by itself and consumes considerable management energy and focus, it is critical to their ability to lease-up and stabilize projects they intend to sell or have presold to institutional investors. In a contrarian move, in 2006 TCR sold its property management company to its employees after deciding that the low margins and the management distraction were no longer worth keeping this capability in house—and after determining that TCR could hire competent property management services from third-party providers. Boston-based John M. Corcoran and Company is unwilling to part with its in-house property management and actually pays itself above-market fees to ensure that its assets are managed "the Corcoran Way." This has been a conscious decision born of the recognition that property management that is better than the market average benefits the company's long-term strategy for holding asset value.

Property managers oversee a wide variety of maintenance services, including cleaning, minor repairs, parking lot maintenance and management, landscape maintenance, and security. Many property management and leasing companies contract out some or all of these services.

Risk. The risks in property management are typically low and limited to working capital and overhead. It can be an intensive human resources challenge, though, given the sheer number of employees involved and the fact that the business tends to have a relatively high degree of employee turnover.

Return. In the past, property managers were well-paid, highly qualified professionals with a finance, legal, accounting, or management background. However, rental property management fees experienced great downward pressure during the 1990s, dropping from an average of 5 percent of annual revenues in the late 1980s to between 2 and 4 percent in 2007. In markets where rents are high, rental apartment property management fees may have fallen below 2 percent. Many third-party property managers have faced extreme profit pressures, which have forced them to become much more efficient. Today, volume is critical, and only control of a large portfolio of properties has allowed operators to flourish economically, benefiting from critical mass to afford standardization systems and lower overhead per unit managed.

Core Competencies. Property managers must possess sophisticated skills in order to profitably handle the multiple demands of the management role. Property management professionals also must have the ability to attract, train, and retain the large numbers of managers and other staff required to manage a portfolio of properties. Property managers who perform maintenance services must have critical knowledge of technical systems and the ability to manage primarily minimum-wage personnel. Maintenance service providers who also act as property managers must be able to manage the inherent conflict of interest that can exist between containing costs, delivering customer service, and enhancing long-term asset value.

Pension Fund Adviser/Pension Fund Consultant

Pension fund advisers acquire and manage real estate assets on behalf of pension funds. They are responsible for structuring the investment plan as well as for administering the pension fund's real estate investments.

Pension fund consultants analyze optimum geographic and product type investments on behalf of a pension fund. They usually oversee the various pension fund advisers who manage the assets of pension fund companies, but they do not actually make the investment or manage the assets owned by the fund.

Risk. The risk to a pension fund adviser is moderate, because of the need for a critical mass of data and modeling capabilities as well as the potential need to invest alongside the pension fund. The risk profile of a pension fund consultant is much lower, because they do not typically coinvest or manage assets.

Return. Depending on the type of investment activity they undertake, compensation for pension fund advisers varies from a low of 0.5 percent to a high of 4 percent, usually with a kicker that is based on the portfolio value or assets under management. Compensation for pension fund consultants tends to run from 0.25 percent to 0.5 percent of the portfolio value.

Core Competencies. Both pension fund advisers and pension fund consultants must have sophisticated market research and portfolio modeling skills, as well as the ability to market to major pension funds in a consolidating business. Pension fund advisers who provide additional services, such as property management, leasing, and so forth, also must be able to manage the inherent conflict of interest.

Make versus Buy

To outsource or not to outsource, that is the question. Decisions regarding a company's industry role strategy also will have significant implications for the company's organizational structure and strategy, which are discussed in more detail in chapter 8. If a company decides to take on a new industry role, it then must decide how to acquire the capabilities needed to take on that role. Will it grow into that role organically, or will it purchase or acquire those capabilities through a merger or acquisition? If an office development firm decides to expand into hotel development, should it recruit and hire people who know how to develop hotels, or should it try to buy or merge with a hotel development company? Mergers and acquisitions can be a more effective and faster route to growth and new industry roles if the target company already has the required core competencies and is playing those roles effectively. There are clear pros and cons to both approaches. The important thing for company leaders to recognize is that how a company goes about taking on new industry roles requires some focused attention.

For example, a company that does third-party construction for others might decide to build only stick-built projects itself and to outsource high-rise or concrete projects, either because it does not have the core competencies required for those types of construction—and does not want to develop them—or because it does not like the risk profile associated with those types of projects. Or it could simply choose not to take on those activities because it recognizes that a competitor already does them better.

Own Account versus Third Party

As a company debates and decides which industry roles it should play, a concurrent step should be to determine for whom the company is going to play these roles. Typically, a company decides to take on a particular activity either only for its own account or for third parties, or sometimes for both. Some real estate develop-

Figure 3-4: INDUSTRY ROLE STRATEGY FOR A REGIONAL HOMEBUILDING COMPANY

INDUSTRY ROLE	Current	Future	New Geography
Land Speculation	Primary/Own Account	Primary/Own Account	Opportunistic/ Own Account
Land Development	No	No	No
Vertical Development	Primary/Own and Third Party	Primary/Own and Third Party	No
Single-Family	Primary/Own Account	Primary/Own Account	Primary/Own Account
Multifamily	Primary/Own Account	Primary/Own Account	Primary/Own Account
Rental Apartments	No	Opportunistic/ Own Account	No
Seniors (50+)	No	No	No
Conversion	No	Primary/Own Account	No
Redevelopment and Reconstruction	No	Primary/Own Account	No
Commercial	No	Opportunistic/ Own Account	No
Mid-Rise/High-Rise Buildings	No	Opportunistic/ Own Account	Opportunistic/ Own Account
Long-Term Investment	No	Opportunistic/ Own Account	Opportunistic/ Own Account

ment and ownership companies decide to take on a particular industry role for third parties only under certain circumstances, and the definition of those circumstances tends to be a product type, a construction type, or a geographic area.

Strategic planners need to look at industry roles as part of a complex, multidimensional matrix of what the company is going to do, for whom, where, and under what circumstances. The picture can get more than a little complicated, but it is important to think about it from the perspective of all these dimensions together.

Figure 3-4 shows an example of an industry role strategy for a regional homebuilder, indicating the roles that the company now undertakes and the ones it intends to pursue, whether they are primary activities (roles for which they will actively plan and develop organizational capabilities), and ones that will remain opportunistic (roles that they will consider but for which they will not consciously develop capabilities during the strategy plan horizon), and for whom (their own account or third parties).

CHAPTER 4

Customer Strategy and Brand

Customer strategies relate to the identification of a company's core customer groups and the attraction, satisfaction, and retention of these core customers. Branding dovetails with a customer strategy and is one of the key defining characteristics of a real estate company's overall strategy.

Customer Definition

At its most basic level, a customer is any individual, group, or entity that pays for, obtains, or uses goods or services from the organization. That person or entity is not necessarily the same as the ultimate end user of the company's goods or services. One party can be a customer for a product or service that ultimately is consumed by another.

Real estate companies typically have multiple customers, both external to the organization and internal, each with its own set of issues and dynamics. Customers typically include end users of goods and services but also may include partners, investors, vendors and suppliers, a host of possible intermediaries, and even employees. For some real estate companies, the primary or most visible customers are buyers and sellers of land; for others, they are buyers and sellers of office, industrial, retail, or apartment buildings; for still others, they are commercial or residential tenants, homebuilders, homebuyers, asset managers, financial institutions, local politicians, company shareholders, stakeholders or investors, and so on.

A company that recognizes and understands each of its customers and constituencies —and has strategies to deal effectively with all of them—will be more successful than one that does not. Conversely, a company that fails to serve one or more of its customers—no matter how well it serves its other constituencies—risks underperforming its competitors.

CUSTOMER DEFINITION

- Who are our customers?
- What do they want and need?
- How can we best satisfy their wants and needs?

Some companies have a fairly clear understanding of their various customers. For some, however, simply going through the exercise of identifying those customers—and gaining clarity on how they differentiate the company from its competition—will be an important phase of the strategic planning process. Defining an effective customer strategy begins by asking the questions listed in the box at left.

AvalonBay Communities is one example of a company that strives to make sure it knows who its residents are and will be. It identifies them by using surveys and focus groups of existing and prospective residents, and by analyzing what sort of impact changing demographics will have on its future resident base. As AvalonBay Communities President and CEO Bryce Blair comments, "We've looked at what the customer's going to look like five years, ten years from now—in terms of them being more diverse in age, more diverse in income, more diverse in ethnicity—and how that would impact the physical product we build for them as well as the services we offer to them. . . . If I hadn't been convinced that the customer would be changing dramatically, I would have been a lot more resistant to making changes in our product line." AvalonBay Communities has expanded beyond its traditional product (suburban wood-frame garden apartment communities) to building townhouses as well as mid-rise and high-rise structures in urban locations and mixed-use developments.

The characteristics of a company's customers—who they are and what they want and need—will help inform and refine the industry role discussion described in chapter 3 (what the company does). They will help a company identify the skills and capabilities, or core competencies, it will need to have in order to succeed (discussed in chapter 5). They will also help the company clarify where, geographically, it should focus its efforts (one of the subjects of chapter 6, which explores growth and geographic deployment strategies). The company that recognizes its customers and is focused on delivering what they desire has a distinct advantage.

Customer-Centric Orientation

Aspirations to be a customer-centric organization (figure 4-1) should form the underpinning of a company's customer-related strategic initiatives. These initiatives should cover two major areas, knowing the customer and delivering the product or service. Knowing the customer involves answering two questions: "Who are our customers?" and "What do they want and need?" in terms of locations, products, and services. Delivering products and services to the customer involves the efficient, effective, and targeted delivery of goods and services, based on an understanding of what customers want and what they are willing to pay for those goods and services.

Figure 4-1: CUSTOMER-CENTRIC ORGANIZATION

For most service-oriented real estate companies, product and service delivery strategies typically center on improving the company's service and ensuring that the company excels at targeted, cost-effective service delivery—the right mix and level of services for the right customer. This does not necessarily mean offering the highest level of customer service regardless of cost but rather matching an appropriate level of customer service to meet that customer's expectations and their ability or willingness to pay. When a customer walks into a Nordstrom store his or her level of expectation regarding customer service is very different than when that same customer walks into a Wal-Mart store—as is his or her willingness to pay a premium or expectation of a discount.

Product-oriented real estate companies such as developers can apply these lessons to the products they provide to ensure that they are delivering the appropriate mix, pricing, and timing of products. This requires a sophisticated, customer-centric system.

Knowing Your Customer

Customer knowledge—and the application of that knowledge—should be the lifeblood of a real estate company's activities and efforts, from submarket and site selection to product design, marketing, and service delivery. Successful companies are those that "get" their customers, that clearly understand who their customers are, what they want and need, where they want and need it, and what they are willing to pay for it. Such companies also understand their customers' motivations and decision-making processes, as well as how their customers want to experience real estate products and services. They create a business culture and processes that are focused on optimizing the overlap between what the customer needs and wants and what the company provides.

Companies must know their customers in order to do the best job possible of delivering to them the products and services they want and need at the highest price and the lowest cost possible. Knowing the customer also can make a company more efficient: a company that knows what its customers want and need can minimize the gap between that and what it offers. It can avoid wasting resources by not offering products, services, or features that its customers do not want or need. Companies that are able to offer customers only what they want and need—and not what they do not want or need—also may be able to charge a premium for those products or services.

KEY CUSTOMER KNOWLEDGE INITIATIVES

- Market research
- Consumer research
- Expert advice

Company leaders therefore should study and learn from their current and likely future customers, and they should ensure that this input guides the company's strategy for the future. Key initiatives that companies can undertake to increase their customer knowledge are described in the box at left.

To institutionalize a culture of customer knowledge, a company must create reliable measurement and monitoring systems to provide an objective view of what its customers perceive. Making optimal use of this customer knowledge will require the company to respect the data as much as its executives' intuition and to avoid wishful thinking, which often leads to irrational exuberance. Implementing the initiatives described in box 10 will enable the company to communicate with and understand its current and targeted customers better. It also will help the company understand what performance needs to be achieved and drive for those results. And it will help build customer loyalty; people like being asked for their opinions and input, and appreciate a chance to help shape products and services.

The End User

One type of customer—the ultimate end user—is particularly important for many real estate companies, though not for all. The ultimate end user is the apartment resident, the homebuyer, the retail shopper, the industrial tenant—the person or entity who ultimately uses the property. In many instances, the company that best understands the end user, even if the end user is not its primary customer, is the one that will have lasting, long-term success. Yet this understanding alone does not guarantee success.

Del Webb Corporation, for example, has done a fabulous job of understanding its end user, the active, 55-plus, retiree homebuyer. Since it opened its first Sun City community near Phoenix in 1960, Del Webb has been offering its homebuyer customers exactly what they want: comfortable, well-built homes in a variety of innovative styles and world-class recreational amenities at an affordable price. Yet Del Webb did not do an effective job of understanding one of its other key customers, its investors. Del Webb was acquired by Pulte Homes in 2001, in part because it was so singularly focused on serving its end-user customer that it did not pay enough attention to its capital source customers. Because Pulte is attuned to the capital markets, the Del Webb brand has continued to succeed and grow since the acquisition. By contrast, real estate companies that choose to ignore the end user—that retain the old attitude of "build it and they will come"—may be surprised when nobody, or the wrong somebody, arrives.

The Intermediary

Many real estate companies have intermediary customers who come between them and their end-user customers (figure 4-2). For a residential land developer, the homebuyer is the end user and the homebuilder is an intermediary; for a shopping center developer, the retail shopper is the end user and the retail tenant is the intermediary. Companies must understand, communicate with, and

Figure 4-2: INTERMEDIARY AND END-USER CUSTOMERS

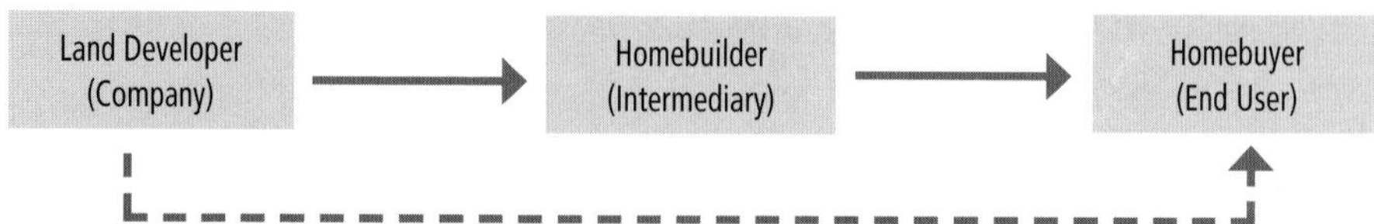

build relationships with both types of customers. In essence, a retail developer must make two sales, one to the shopper and one to the retail tenant. Understanding the end users (target homebuyers) should help a land developer select the right intermediaries (homebuilders) and inform those homebuilders about the target homebuyers, resulting in a better relationship between the developer and the homebuilders. That relationship is what ultimately will deliver a better product and experience—for which homebuyers will be willing to pay a premium. Therefore the homebuilders should be willing to pay more for the land, and the developer should maximize its returns. Likewise, retail developers must first care about target shoppers, perhaps even more than they care about their primary customer, the retail tenant. They must first understand the needs and wants of the shoppers they aim to attract and then bring in the right retailers to attract and serve that customer base.

Real estate companies that do not understand their end-user customers and that bring in intermediaries (homebuilders or retailers, in the above examples) without considering the end user do so in hopes that the intermediaries will attract the right customers. If they have chosen successful intermediaries, the customers will come, but they may not be the optimal customers from the developer's perspective. When developers fail to understand the end user, they give up an element of control to their intermediaries; in essence, they allow the intermediaries—or chance—to determine who their end users will be, which generally does not enable developers to maximize profits.

Visionary real estate companies often seem able to foresee what their customers will need and want—and where they will want it—even before the customers realize these things. By understanding their end-user customers so well, these companies are able to recognize opportunities that others may not see, to develop innovative new projects in pioneering locations, and to attract intermediaries and, ultimately, end users to those projects.

The Scottsdale, Arizona–based Lyle Anderson Company is one example of a visionary, customer-focused company that recognized what its customers—affluent baby boomer retirees—would want even before they did (and well before they became retirees). As writer Richard Hoffer put it, "Anderson's genius isn't simply building world-class communities on land once thought worthless. It's knowing what we want years before we know what we want."[1] Anderson began buying up land in the Arizona desert in the late 1970s—when the leading edge of the boomer generation was only 29 years old—in anticipation of those boomers' retirement years. Three years into his investment, seeing the long waiting lists for membership at Phoenix-area golf clubs, he realized that soon there would be a huge market for communities in which everyone who bought a home could also purchase a club membership, with no wait. Anderson's Phoenix area communities, which include Desert Highlands, Desert Mountain, and Superstition Mountain, offer just that, as well as the luxury homes and other amenities and services sought out by leisure-minded affluent retirees.

Product and Service Delivery

The customer service element of a real estate company's customer strategy should center on improving how the company delivers what its customers want and ensuring that the company provides appropriate, cost-effective, and targeted service to all of its customers, including both end users and intermediaries. Key strategic initiatives in this process should include at least those described in the following sections.

Organization

First, a company needs to create organizational capabilities, allocate resources to champion key customer service initiatives, and benchmark and measure progress. Merely declaring a "customer focus" will not suffice; a company must invest time and energy in institutionalizing a customer focus, or it will not happen. Some companies have gone so far as to create a new senior position (such as a vice president of customer service), conduct organizational reviews of the way they deliver customer service, and suggest modifications to enhance customer service delivery. By whatever means the company determines most effective, it must put in place mechanisms to identify key roadblocks and strategize how to improve customer service. The company also should tie some of its employees' compensation to customer delivery goals. (See chapter 8 for more details.)

Training and Process

The company should determine its customers' expectations and develop service standards designed to meet those expectations. It may create a "service statement" to communicate its service standards to employees and customers. It may reevaluate and revise all its communications with customers. When hiring and training new employees, it may decide to focus on hiring customer-centric staff and may provide customer service training.

Research and Monitoring

The company may choose to conduct a variety of research and monitoring activities, such as consumer research (including resident, tenant, or buyer satisfaction surveys, focus groups, and move-in/move-out surveys), peer group customer satisfaction surveys, mystery shops, and maintenance operations evaluations.

One of the great sources of inefficiency and lost profit opportunities is delivering goods or services that customers value at prices that are less than the cost of delivery. As with customer knowledge initiatives, these product and service initiatives can help a company determine what its customers value and what they do not value, and how well the company does in satisfying its customers. Consequently, the business will be better able to meet its customers' expectations, to provide what they need and want and—just as important—to avoid wasting resources by providing what they do not want or need (or do not value enough).

AvalonBay Communities is one example of a company that has made customer focus a key element of its strategy. In 2002, the company's leaders elected to modify AvalonBay's mission statement. Previously, the company's statement was largely about the "bricks and sticks" aspect of their apartment development and management business: "We build great communities." The new mission statement emphasizes customer knowledge and delivery: "Enhancing the lives of our residents."

DMB Associates, Inc., a Scottsdale-based diversified investment and development company focused on large-scale resort/recreation and primary home and commercial developments in Arizona, California, Hawaii, and Utah, is another example of a customer-focused company that has made a strategic commitment to understanding and anticipating the needs of its multiple customer markets and delivering what both they and the surrounding community's residents want. With foresight, creativity, and appreciation for the amenities and community life its customer base is seeking, DMB is in a position to command a premium price for the opportunity to build or buy in one of its highly sought-after communities. One of the interesting approaches the company has brought to its developments is a commitment to having residents realize its vision early in the development life cycle, with the construction of the core amenities in place as the projects are launched.

The company's vision and commitment to quality have been the underpinning for establishing and maintaining long-term partnerships with homebuilders. Indeed, partnership is one of DMB's core values and is evidenced by the long-term relationships that the company enjoys with its consultant and vendor partners as well. DMB is highly recognized within the industry and sought out by landowners who have special places they want to develop with DMB. DMB's four core values of legacy, partnership, profit, and fun are the foundation of its growth and success and fundamental to the way this company serves its customer base.

Similarly, the Lyle Anderson Company, the Arizona-based developer of large-scale premier golf communities in Arizona, New Mexico, and Hawaii, has cultivated a customer-focused culture that drives its location, design, and marketing efforts. By understanding its customer—the high-end golfer who is looking for an exclusive and high-service experience—the company is able to charge a premium for its offerings, often attracting customers who purchase lots and memberships in various locations, as well as upgrade within a given community over time.

Customer loyalty is an important goal of the customer strategies of many real estate companies. Customer loyalty results in referrals, retention, reduced costs to service, increased cross-selling opportunities, and increased revenue and profits. Building a reputation for excellence and branding are two ways to build customer loyalty.

Branding

What is a brand? Although the American Marketing Association defines a brand as "a name, term, sign, symbol, or any other feature that identifies one seller's goods or services as distinct from those of another seller's," the term has come to mean much more. Brands in the 21st century are more than mere symbols. A brand communicates a mass of information about a company, a product, or a service; it conveys to customers the specific personality, the attitude, the lifestyle that the brand represents. One of the benefits of a successful customer strategy is that, in many cases, it can result in a recognizable and successful brand, one that encourages customers to suspend normal due diligence activities and enables a company to garner market share or charge premium pricing for its products and services.

Branding is a widely recognized competitive advantage in the hotel sector. Elsewhere in the real estate industry, there is vigorous debate about the effectiveness of branding, and whether the return on investment is sufficient. Proponents say a brand can effectively differentiate a real estate company from others in the industry by encapsulating that company's identity and what it promises to deliver to its customers. Likewise, a brand can differentiate a building, a community, or a neighborhood from others and thus attract and retain a specific set of customers or market segment. One of the benefits of having a brand is that it may encourage customers and others to suspend due diligence procedures that they normally would undertake before entering into a transaction. Landowners may sell a company land, governments may grant greater approvals or entitlements (or grant them faster, with fewer restrictions), office tenants may lease space and homebuyers may purchase homes at high prices or at a faster rate, all because a company has a recognizable and respected brand. Likewise, during a downturn in the real estate cycle or the general economy, real estate companies with recognized and respected brands are able to maintain a greater than fair share of whatever activity remains in the market. A brand also can offer benefits in the capital markets: a company with a respected brand can attract capital more easily and possibly on more favorable terms than a company without the same level of brand awareness. Finally, a brand also can attract human capital talent to the company, potentially a critical advantage.

Detractors say that real estate is unlike many other consumer products, such as cars or bars of soap. As outlined above, with the exception of the hotel and, perhaps, the self-storage segments, where brand has been used effectively and does make a real difference in consumer decisions, real estate transactions are relatively few and they are spread over a long period of time. A consumer may make a decision to rent an apartment two or three times over the course of his or her lifetime, and office tenants typically move every ten years or so. Other factors, such as location and price, are much more important than brand in these types of decisions. These factors, it is argued, makes it difficult to build a real estate brand and to benefit from that brand.

Did Equity Office have a brand, and did tenants overlook competing space or pay more to rent space in an Equity office building than in a building without a brand? Clearly the private equity fund Blackstone, which purchased Equity Office, did not think the brand had much value, because it broke up the portfolio and sold it off in chunks to the highest bidders in various markets.

Yet many are convinced that successful branding programs can increase revenues and sales, trigger customer loyalty, elevate a company or a project's standing within the community, trigger economic growth, and enrich the public domain. More and more real estate companies are beginning to brand their products and services, and their experiences offer some lessons for others.

The leaders of Boston Properties are convinced that there is power in branding office properties. They believe the company can gain a competitive advantage in the Class A office market by understanding and meeting the demands of high-quality tenants who require more sophisticated infrastructure and support services. Branding for Boston Properties means becoming a "landlord of choice," and the company has invested heavily in providing consistently superior in-house building management expertise that enables them to react to, and even anticipate, tenants' needs. The company claims that practicing this strategy enables it to retain high-quality tenants at market or above-market rates and builds brand loyalty.

Empirically, we know that certain companies enjoy better prices, absorption, and occupancy levels and obtain better terms than others, and it is difficult not to attribute such superior performance to brand value. AvalonBay Communities, DMB, Lyle Anderson, and others certainly believe in the value of their brands.

Harry Frampton, managing partner of East West Partners, is a strong believer in the value of the company's brand and brand recognition, which the company has found to be particularly powerful in securing entitlements and getting the political machinery to move to approve its projects. Many people believe that nobody other than East West Partners, perhaps because of its corporate brand identity, could have secured the entitlements it received for the destination resort it is building in North Lake Tahoe, and that probably nobody will ever be able to secure such entitlements again. Yet East West Partners ultimately decided that "place" was more important to the project's ultimate end users (homebuyers and club members) and therefore created a separate brand name, Tahoe Mountain Resorts, for the resort's four communities and its club. Similarly, DMB finds that its corporate brand and reputation help it gain entitlements and attract both financial and human capital, but the firm uses separate brand names for each of its communities—including Ladera Ranch, Santaluz, and DC Ranch—many of which have become respected, well-recognized brands on their own. Neither firm hides its involvement with any of its projects, but both ensure that the place name is more prominent (in signage, marketing materials, and the like) than the corporate name.

AvalonBay Communities also has spent a great deal of time thinking about the value of its brand. Chairman and CEO Blair does not view branding as a financial investment; rather, he sees it as a major organizational investment, in the sense that much of the work of brand building involves delivering a consistent package to the customer. These are things that the company must deliver, notes Blair, whether it engages in branding or not: "You have to name a community anyway, you have to put up a sign, you have to have collateral material, you have to build a physical product. So tying all that into a package with consistent names, signage, advertising, colors and logos, and service guarantees is really pretty cheap in dollar terms. The big investment is in spending the time to try to understand what you want your brand to stand for and trying to ingrain that into your organization."

Blair believes that AvalonBay's branding effort has a major impact on how all of its customers—not just its end-user customer, the resident—view its communities. "Where we have a large market presence—in Boston or San Jose or Washington, D.C., for example," says Blair, "the power of the brand is without debate, not just with our [residents] but with prospective employees, who know AvalonBay Communities and want to work for an industry leader, with our existing associates, who take great pride in seeing our name everywhere and wearing the company logo, with the subcontractors who want to work for a company that's well known and well respected. . . with the municipalities with which we do business, because [our ability to] consistently deliver a product reduces risks for a municipality as well. So our brand gives us a tremendous leg up [on the competition]."

Development companies have a big advantage in the branding process, notes Blair: "We're building our portfolio every day, so we can incorporate design elements into each of our new communities." For real estate companies acquiring existing assets, he notes, "just putting up a new sign may not be worth the money."

A company also may find it essential to protect established brand identities and reputations as it expands and moves into new market segments. The Bozzuto Group made a conscious decision to operate its LIHTC rental apartment portfolio under a different brand name. It did this for two reasons: first, to avoid damaging its Class A apartment business, in terms of name recognition both with end users (renters) and with owners and investors, and second, to keep the Class A business "pure" from an internal perspective. It wanted to make sure its own employees—and prospective new talent—understood the differences in how the two separate and independent companies were managed.

Trammell Crow Residential undertook a branding effort that included consistent naming toward the end of the 1990s (the company had undertaken some regional branding efforts before that). One of the reasons was that its leaders thought doing so would save on marketing costs. The company also built affordable tax-credit apartments under a different brand name, just as Bozzuto has.

It is important for company leaders to debate the issue of brand and decide what, if anything, the company is going to do about it. How much of an impact could the right brand have on the company and its products? Could the brand affect customer decisions? Could end users (homebuyers, apartment residents, office tenants) recognize and differentiate between real estate brands? Are projects by branded companies better able to withstand pricing pressures than those by nonbranded ones? How does brand differ from reputation? What could be the benefits of branding?

At a minimum, efforts to create a brand also create efficiencies and economies of scale that can have a very real impact on profitability. An apartment, office, or retail company that is able to market its portfolio of properties in a marketplace under a single brand name can have a bigger impact and can make more efficient media purchases for newspaper ads. Efforts to brand and enhance a company's reputation may make it easier to secure development rights in an increasingly difficult entitlement environment, and companies with an established brand may indeed secure "first call" status from land sellers and capital providers. In some cases, a brand can translate into pricing power. Post Properties in Atlanta and Charles E. Smith Residential Realty in Crystal City (northern Virginia) each have had such a concentrated portfolio, such a dominant presence, that each was able to dictate pricing—at least to some degree—in those markets. In fact, the Charles E. Smith brand was so strong that even after the company merged with Archstone Communities to become Archstone-Smith in 2001, the new firm retained the original brand name.

Master-planned community developers Lyle Anderson and DMB also believe that their projects get price and absorption premiums beyond those of their competitors as a result of brand recognition. Likewise, in the office business, companies such as Arden Realty and the Irvine Company in southern California and Spieker Properties (which was acquired by Equity Office Properties Trust in 2001) in northern California all get a premium for having brand names that are associated with better-quality projects, better property and asset management, and better customer service. Even in a competitive market, companies with well-known, respected brands have their pick of tenants, who believe they will get better treatment and are making a safer investment by renting from such companies and are willing to pay a premium to do so.

Real estate companies that decide to develop a brand strategy must ensure that the brand clearly and accurately reflects the company and its strategic goals. A company's brand must be aligned with reality; customers will quickly recognize (and devalue the brand of) companies that claim to be what they are not or that fail to deliver the brand promise. Once a company creates a realistic and positive brand concept, it should ensure that all of its actions and messages—including signage, advertising, press releases, events, and so forth—are "on brand." Continually reinforcing and communicating a company's brand concept with employees, customers, partners, investors, and others will help align the organization behind strategic objectives and differentiate the company in what may be an increasingly competitive environment. The brand becomes one of the company's most cherished and guarded assets, one of its most valued core competencies, and it is fiercely protected against internal or external violations.

Is branding really worth the investment in time and money? The answer is still "it depends." As AvalonBay's Blair comments, "It depends on what the company's strategy is. If you don't have the scale [to make it worthwhile] in a given submarket, I wouldn't do it. If you don't have the ability to have a relatively homogeneous product, I wouldn't do it. If you're not committed to providing exceptional service, I wouldn't do it. You need to have all of those elements working together." When all of those elements are working together, Blair firmly believes that branding has an impact on a property's and a company's overall performance. "I think [the benefit] comes in a number of different areas," he notes. "It reduces our marketing expenditures, because we can leverage those expenditures better. It also allows the prospective resident to make a decision more quickly. And if residents have a positive experience [with the brand], they're going to be less price sensitive. We still need to be competitive, but I think the brand allows us to charge a premium price for our product and services."

Blair warns that it is possible for a company to have negative brand equity, describing a letter he received from a dissatisfied resident who told him, "Every time someone asks me about an AvalonBay community, I'll be sure to tell them how unhappy I was." Customers' negative experiences are magnified as much as—or even more than—positive ones, so a company that fails to deliver on its brand's promise will suffer the consequences.

What is the bottom line as far as customer strategy and branding are concerned? A company that has a well-articulated customer strategy and is able to create an effective brand should excel in getting the "first call" for deals and talent, receive better treatment from government agencies, be able to obtain favorable pricing and terms from vendors and capital sources, and enjoy better pricing power or velocity than its competitors, enabling it to do better than its competitors at all times but particularly when times are tough.

Endnote

[1] Hoffer, Richard, "The Desert Fox," *Golf Connoisseur*, Summer 2005, 92–97.

CHAPTER 5

Core Competency Strategy

Armed with a solid mission and vision, an understanding of the industry roles that it intends to pursue, and a clear definition of its customer and brand, a company then needs to go about defining the critical capabilities that it needs to develop, maintain, or acquire to succeed. In short, what are going to be the company's critical core competencies?

Core competencies are skills or assets of a company that enable it to be better, faster, or cheaper than its competition, thus giving it a competitive advantage in the marketplace. A company that does not have any core competencies probably is not going to be around for long. Without core competencies, a company is relegated to playing a relatively minor role in its industry. Having a core competency means that the firm has, or intends to have, clear superiority over its competition or its peer group in mission-critical areas.

If you ask people what their company does incredibly well, they generally will list ten or 20 items. Company leaders engaged in the strategic planning process should challenge themselves to focus on just a handful of critical core competencies—no more than five. Whenever possible, the core competencies that a firm either has and wants to maintain or wants to build should be defined as the most critical things that the company must do to propel the business, differentiate it in the often crowded marketplace, and enable it to achieve its strategic objectives.

Cherokee Investment Partners is an excellent example of a company that understands its critical core competencies and is focused exclusively on what it can be the best in the world at—brownfield redevelopment. Since the company's inception in 1993, Cherokee's model has been the acquisition and reclamation of "impaired assets," which it returns to productive use in the United States and Western Europe. Its core philosophy is to promote the sustainable redevelopment of contaminated sites in order to provide net positive social, economic, and environmental improvements. The company has historically been a horizontal land developer, its expertise centered on acquiring, remediating, and selling clean entitled sites to vertical developers and builders.

One of Cherokee's key core competencies is the ability to take on projects that other investors or developers typically reject. Cherokee understands the environmental, legal, and political environments better than most and can underwrite the environmental risks that most developers find uncomfortable. While others are just getting their feet wet in sustainable development, Cherokee has a proven track record of transforming communities where urban blight and environmental contamination have impeded economic growth and community redevelopment. As the company says on its Web site, "In conjunction with placing capital and generating returns for our investors, we provide solutions for sellers and the cities affected by their contaminated sites. Cherokee typically acquires assets for cash and indemnifies the seller from environmental liability through the use of insurance policies and other customized risk methods."

Existing Core Competencies

The first step in developing a company's core competencies is to identify its existing ones. What does the company do better, faster, or cheaper than its competitors today? Where does it have competitive advantages (or disadvantages) in the marketplace? Do its core competencies actually make a difference? The best way to begin to identify a company's strengths and weaknesses is to compare it with its relevant peer group or competition. The ranking scale used in the box on page 76 can be helpful.

Using a scale from 1 to 5, a company can compare its position relative to that of the competition along those dimensions that company leaders deem most relevant. Although each company and situation is different, most real estate companies tend to define critical core competencies in five major categories:

■ *Reputation/Brand.* The ability to maintain "first call" status with land or building sellers, brokers, partners, capital sources, and talent—defined as being on the short list of companies that are routinely contacted first, before opportunities are widely disseminated to the marketplace;

■ *Customer Focus/Marketing.* The ability to understand customers and their needs, and then to deliver the appropriate product in a timely manner;

■ *Construction.* The ability to deliver a high-quality product on time and on budget;

CORE COMPETENCY RATING AND DEFINITION

5 = Better than virtually every other company in this area—a clear competitive advantage

4 = Better than most companies; a handful of competitors may also have this competency—may be a competitive advantage

3 = On par with relevant competitors—neither a competitive advantage nor a competitive disadvantage in the marketplace

2 = Most competitors are better—may be a competitive disadvantage

1 = Virtually all relevant competitors are better in this area—a clear competitive disadvantage

■ *Finance.* The ability to obtain and deploy capital; and

■ *Organization.* The ability to retain a well-motivated and appropriately structured and staffed organization that operates efficiently and profitably.

It is important to examine all the company's core competencies. Company leaders then need to identify which core competencies are most important for the company's future—those that will actually facilitate meaningful competitive advantage—because some core competencies may not be as relevant as others. Company leaders must figure out the areas on which the company should focus, by either maintaining or improving itself to the point at which it earns a relative ranking of 4 or 5. This does not mean the company should not be competent at a lot of other things. Committing to focus on developing or maintaining critical core competencies in three to five areas does not mean that a company's leaders can ignore the company's other capabilities or vast swathes of its business. But company leaders may decide that in some areas it will be perfectly acceptable for the company to be on par with others.

For example, a developer of high-end resort residential products may determine that being a first call for land sellers, customer knowledge, sales and marketing, and construction quality are absolutely essential. Therefore, these are core competencies on which the company must rate a 5 in order to succeed. But that developer may also determine that having the absolute lowest cost of capital down to the nearest ten basis points, while nice, is not essential. The company cannot be at a significant disadvantage with regard to its cost of capital, but perhaps it is fine to be at parity with its relevant competition and rate a 3 on this dimension. Deciding on core competencies is about identifying the few things that really make the company special, that differentiate it from other firms, that help it succeed and move to the front of the pack, or that are requisite to an industry sector (or segment) leadership position.

Gap Analysis

As a company goes about the exercise of rating itself on the core competencies its leaders have identified as critical for its continuing success, important areas where the company does not yet have a competitive advantage will come into focus. The issue of core competencies will arise again and again throughout the strategic planning process, as a company makes important decisions about its industry roles, growth strategies, and geographic deployment (the subject of the next chapter). As it decides to take on new roles or expand into new markets or product segments, a company will have to revisit and possibly refine its chosen critical core competencies. Executives should be careful not to let a company's existing core competencies, or the lack thereof, determine the company's strategy—again, at least not initially. For example, a company in the rental apartment business may have critical core competencies that make it fabulous at building and leasing up apartment projects, but it may not have general contracting capabilities. If the company sees an opportunity to perform that function—either for itself or for third parties—its lack of a core competency in this area should not, in itself, be the reason it decides not to go into that business.

General Growth Properties (GGP) is one example of a company that decided to try something different and is doing it successfully, even though it did not initially have the capabilities needed. An owner, developer, and manager of shopping centers since 1954, GGP merged with the Rouse Company in 2004 and is increasing density and adding residential development at many of its retail properties. The company hired experienced residential talent, bringing people in house in order to expand GGP's core competencies into residential and mixed-use development. Another retail developer, New England Development, took the opposite approach and has been equally successful in expanding its capabilities by partnering with other companies—for example, joining a joint venture with Archstone-Smith to do the residential development and Boston Properties to do the office development at its large-scale Wisconsin Place mixed-use project in Chevy Chase, Maryland—while maintaining its focus on retail development.

Executives should avoid the knee-jerk reaction, "But we don't know how to do that!" The company could choose to develop a core competency in an area by hiring skilled construction managers or by acquiring or partnering with an established general contracting firm. Likewise, a company that has developed a strategic plan that sets out its aspirations for the future will need to examine that plan in the context of its existing core competencies; determine which core competencies it needs to maintain, shore up, or acquire in order to realize its aspirations; and then move forward from there.

Define, Benchmark, and Measure

Once a company has identified a short list of core competencies that are essential to its strategy, it should define, benchmark, and measure its progress toward achieving the desired relative rankings on those core competencies.

First, a company should define in concrete terms what it means to have a core competency in a particular area. Simply declaring that the company has a core competency is insufficient. A company might need to define, for example, what it means to have a critical core competency in property management; it might decide that it will rate a 5 in property management when it achieves certain key criteria. Perhaps being "the best rental apartment property manager" could be defined as having the ability to charge high rents, enjoy lower turnover, generate strong net operating income, or command higher fees for third-party property management services than other companies.

The second step is to determine the relevant metric that should be used to measure a core competency, in order to know whether a company has achieved it or not. If "we're the best property managers" means that the company is able to charge higher fees for its third-party property management services or has a lower resident turnover rate than other companies, the means of measuring whether a company has a core competency in property management become clear: How do the firm's property management service fees or resident turnover rates compare with those of the competition? Coming up with a metric that can be used to know whether a company has a specific core competency—a way to measure and benchmark where the firm is today and how its performance improves on a particular core competency—is critical.

Ideally, the company should find a metric that enables it to benchmark itself against its relevant peer group or industry. This has been made somewhat easier with the number of publicly traded real estate companies and the increasing amount of data available about the real estate market, but it is not always possible or economically viable to obtain peer-level data to benchmark every relevant metric. In these cases, the next-best thing a company can do is benchmark and set measurements and goals for improving its performance that are based on internally generated metrics. For example, a company may not be able to get resident turnover data for its peer group in a given marketplace, but it certainly can benchmark its own resident turnover and set goals to improve.

The third step is to put strategies or actions in place that enable the company to maintain, shore up, or attain those core competencies. These are concrete steps that the company should put in place to improve on the chosen benchmark metrics.

These three steps give company leaders the tools they need to come to a consensus and say, "yes, we agree that this is where the company is today, we agree on where it needs to be in the future, and we're not just going to wave our arms and say 'we need to do better.' We're going to put actual strategies in place to get from where we are to where we need to be." A company may decide, for example, that it wants to develop a core competency in property management. It may rank its current competency in that area at 2 or 3 but decide that the company's strategy makes it essential to become a 5. As long as it is able to define for itself what it means to have a core competency in property management

Figure 5-1: CORE COMPETENCIES STRATEGY

Competency	Current	Goal
■ Customer Focus	2	5
• Market Knowledge	3	5
• Market/Selling	3	4
■ Financial Resources	3	4
■ Human Capital	2	5
■ Reputation and Relationships	3	5
■ Land Strategy	4	5
■ Implementation Expertise	3	4
■ Company Culture	4	5
■ Community Outreach	5	5
■ Brand	3	4
■ Operational Excellence	3	4
■ Internal Communication	3	4
■ Effective Delegation	3	3
■ Leadership Skills	3	4
■ Teamwork	3	4

FOCUS (Customer Focus through Implementation Expertise)

Scale:
5 = Competitive Advantage
4 = Clear Competency
3 = Parity
2 = Lack Competency
1 = Disadvantage

and can identify several ways to measure its progress in that area, the company will vastly improve its chances of actually achieving its objectives.

Figure 5-1 illustrates the result of a company's conclusions about its core competency strategy. It outlines the dozen or so elements that were deemed important for the company to be successful, along with an assessment of the status that the company is achieving on each dimension. Further, it illustrates the six items that the company determined were absolutely critical in order for it to achieve its strategic objectives over the planning horizon. The strategy team members knew that they could not ignore the items at the bottom of the list and that they were going to set specific action items to maintain and improve the company's core competencies on the top six elements, then benchmark them, and measure progress toward achieving the desired outcome.

CHAPTER 6

Growth and Geographic Deployment Strategy

During the upturn and mature phases of the real estate cycle, growth naturally becomes the major focus of any real estate company. During downturns, many service businesses turn their attention to growth as well, either by targeting new customers or by adding new services to their existing customer base. For example, in a downturn, property management and asset management service providers may begin to focus on providing workout services to institutional owners of troubled properties.

Just like it sounds, growth strategy refers to a set of strategies related to business growth. These strategies typically focus on expanding the two primary factors—geographic market and product or service segment—described below. Growth strategies are designed to improve a company's economic performance by leveraging its resources in a manner that creates the lowest risk while providing the highest return. As a company plans its growth, it should build on its strengths (where risk is lowest) and minimize compounding risks by minimizing the need to rely on capital, knowledge, systems, or human resources that it currently lacks.

The risk associated with growth relates to the exposure that the company accepts in order to facilitate growth. This risk can be viewed both in terms of the capital required to fund the growth and in terms of how the company's systems and human resources must be stretched to accept the additional workload associated with the growth.

Growth strategies typically range from low-risk/low-growth to high-risk/high-growth strategies (figure 6-1). The lowest-risk growth strategy is the market penetration strategy, in which the company focuses on doing what it already knows how to do and simply tries to increase its share of available local demand by capitalizing on its customer knowledge, brand name, local reputation, and economies of scale. This strategy calls for staying in the same geographic market(s), serving the same customer segment(s), building the same product(s), or offering the same services. The highest-risk growth strategy is the new business strategy, which calls for a company to enter one or more new geographic markets, address a new customer segment, and offer new products or services.

Figure 6-1: GROWTH STRATEGY

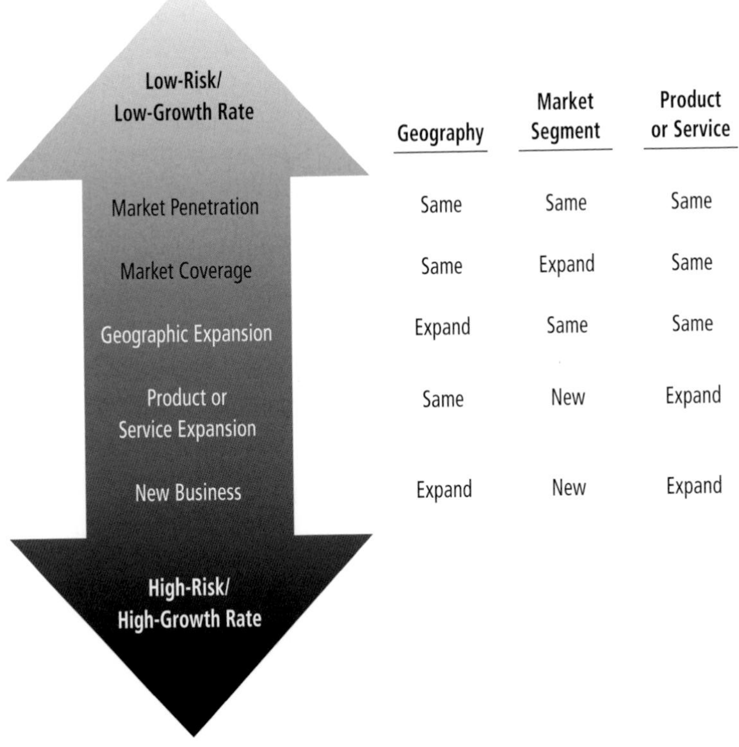

How and Where a Company Grows

Two major factors determine the growth strategy for a real estate company: geographic market and product or service segment.

Geographic Market

The geographic market is the area or areas in which the company conducts business. Most real estate companies define their geographic deployment in terms of metropolitan areas or regions. This is logical, because each metropolitan area is a single economic unit driven by a unique set of "export" industries' and other factors that stimulate job and household growth within the region. The real estate market is, in turn, driven by that growth.

Product or Service Segment

Product types include all familiar real estate property types: office, industrial, residential, hotel, retail, and the rest. Real estate service types include brokerage, management, consulting, and other service categories.

The phases of the real estate cycle frequently do not coincide for various product types. One product type may be in an upturn while another may be in a downturn. This enables companies to focus on those product types that offer the most promise during each phase. For example, in the early years of the 21st century, the fundamentals for new development of many income-producing property products were not favorable. The opposite was true for for-sale residential products, and many commercial and rental apartment developers took advantage of this situation by becoming quite active in the for-sale housing business. By 2005 this situation had reversed, as also happened in the 1980s, when income-producing products came back very early in the upturn phase but for-sale housing lagged considerably behind in many markets. For example, when the Washington, D.C., metropolitan area office market died in the late 1980s, the Artery Group returned to its roots as a rental apartment developer, adding residential land development capabilities in the 1990s and retail and hotel development in the first decade of the 21st century. At the end of the most recent cycle, the company sold the bulk of its income-producing portfolio as capitalization rates dipped to historical lows and in 2007 was positioning itself for the next upturn.

Segments are subcategories within each product or service type. Retail product segments include convenience centers (small, unanchored), neighborhood centers (grocery and drug store–anchored), community and power centers (anchored by big-box stores and discounters), specialty and festival centers (unanchored, high-end, focused on entertainment, apparel, and restaurants), regional and super regional malls (large, internally oriented, department store–anchored), outlet malls (anchored by off-price factory outlets), lifestyle centers (upscale, open-air shopping venues that often contain a mix of other uses), and individual pad sites (for fast-food restaurants and banks, among other users). Industrial, office, hotel, residential, and recreational uses all are characterized by a vast array of product segments as well. Likewise, management service segments include construction management, development management, portfolio management, asset management, and property management functions.

Growth Strategies and Attendant Risk Profiles

When these two major factors—geographic market and product or service segment—are placed into the matrix shown in figure 6-2, four basic growth strategies emerge. Each strategy has a different risk characteristic, as outlined below.

Market Penetration Strategy: Same Product or Service, Same Market

The market penetration growth strategy focuses on the same geographic market(s), same product or service type(s), and same product or service

Figure 6-2: MARKET AND PRODUCT OR SEGMENT RISK PROFILES

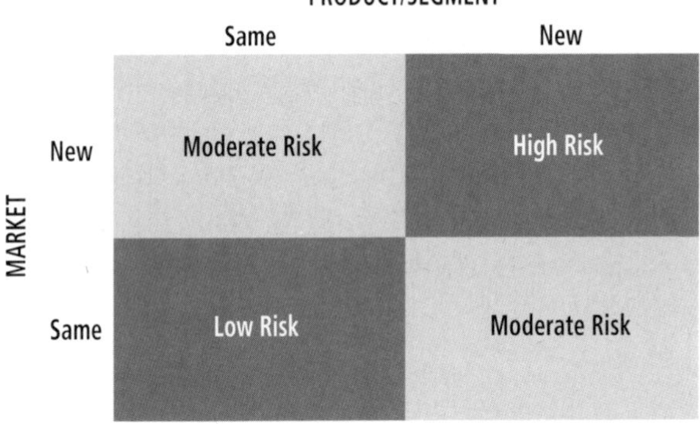

segment(s) that the company has emphasized in the past. In essence, the company plans to do "more of the same" but to absorb a greater market share—something that many real estate companies do not realize is possible even when the opportunity is right in front of them. Like many business executives, real estate executives often fall prey to the myth that "the grass is always greener on the other side of the fence."

When executives at Trico Homes began a strategic planning exercise in preparation for a planned expansion, they believed they needed to move into new geographic markets in order to grow. As they were challenged to examine the company's penetration of its core market in Calgary, they realized that they could capture more of the market share there—at a lower risk—before expanding north to Edmonton. AvalonBay Communities' decision to be more focused geographically in fewer markets was an outgrowth of a strategic effort to explore whether being in more markets really provided greater diversification. After careful consideration and analysis the answer was no, it did not, and that gave the company the direction to concentrate its investments in fewer markets.

Market penetration offers the lowest risk of all growth strategies. It eliminates the uncertainties associated with unknown entitlements, construction, or marketing factors and thus permits the real estate company to focus on what it presumably does best. Few real estate companies push against the existing limits of growth in any particular market. Only when a company begins to compete with itself (for example, by putting pressure on its lease rates, sale prices, or absorption, because of its own nearby projects) does it approach its natural growth limits.

Market Expansion Strategy: Same Product or Service, New Market

The market expansion strategy allows the company to build on its product or service expertise (its core competency in product knowledge) and take a proven product or service on the road. The real estate company moves a specific product or product segment that already has met with tremendous success into new markets whose economic, demographic, and political characteristics are similar to those of the home market. Formula restaurant, hotel, and retail chains frequently use this expansion strategy, as do some real estate companies. Service businesses also can use this strategy of moving existing services to new markets.

In the middle of the first decade of the 21st century, Florida-based WCI Communities decided to take its 50 years of expertise in land development, homebuilding, and high-rise development in the Florida market and expand into the northeastern and mid-Atlantic markets, through acquisitions of Spectrum Communities, which operated in New York, Connecticut, and New Jersey, in 2004 and Renaissance Housing, which operated in Maryland and Virginia, in 2005. There are now more than 50 WCI communities in six states.

When deciding which new markets they should enter, a number of companies look to markets where supply is constrained or barriers to entry are high. Although it may be more difficult to penetrate these types of markets, companies reason that it is better to be in a location with limited competition and limited opportunities to develop than it is to go to places—like the Southeast or Southwest—where there is far more competition and it is far easier to overbuild the marketplace.

Although the risk associated with moving into a new market is not as low as that associated with the market penetration growth strategy, it is close. The product or service markets are so well known that firms have little difficulty finding the best locations in a new geographic market. Once the concept has been proven, however, other companies may overbuild or overserve the market.

Product or Service Expansion Strategy: New Product or Service, Same Market

With the third growth strategy, the company builds on its market expertise (its core competency in market knowledge) and takes on a new product, product segment, or service type within a known geographic market. In other words, it stays home but learns how to develop or service a new product type or product segment.

Examples of companies that have chosen this strategy abound. On the product side, national homebuilder Toll Brothers tried entering the rental apartment business in the Washington, D.C., market, where it already was building for-sale housing, but this venture did not work out very well. Conversely, JPI, principally a rental apartment developer and manager with divisions throughout the United States, got into the for-sale condominium business in a big way when the cycle for that product was strong, both in Washington, D.C., and elsewhere.

Other companies have expanded by increasing their service offerings. The Bozzuto Group added a landscaping business, originally to serve its own properties, that later became a thriving independent operation through contracts with military bases and other landowners. Bozzuto's property management company, which also was started to provide services to Bozzuto projects, later grew into a third-party provider and now manages more assets that are not owned by Bozzuto than are. East West Partners, which at its core is a land development company, acquired and expanded several synergistic service companies to help it penetrate the Vail Valley market, including a transportation company (which ferries visitors from area airports to the company's resorts), a resort management company, a property and asset management company, a brokerage business (which now sells more property in the Vail Valley than any other company), and a technology business that provides marketing technology solutions for both its own and outside real estate projects. When deciding which new service business to enter and maintain, East West Partners used the criterion of synergy: the service had to relate to or reinforce the company's core land development business. What all these businesses have in common (with the exception of the technology business, which East West Partners later jettisoned because it did not add value to the organization's ventures) is the customer. The people flying into Denver who need transportation to Vail are the same people looking to purchase or rent property developed, managed, or sold by East West Partners.

This growth strategy—product or service expansion—enables a company to pursue a balanced portfolio strategy and to spread costs and risks over product types that have different cycles. In addition, the firm can expand its operations without traveling or learning about new geographic markets. The probability of achieving synergistic benefits with existing product types is great. On the downside, however, companies face the risk that a major recession will hit their metropolitan area and compromise the performance of all real estate product types or services, resulting in too many eggs in one basket. Furthermore, entering a new product field poses a double-edged danger. One is that some companies erroneously assume that existing management can be retrofitted to meet the new challenges. The other is that new senior-level talent recruited to move the firm into the new product segment may not fit into the corporate culture. Delivering a new product segment rather than an entirely new product—as happened, for example, when a developer of budget hotels in the Chicago suburbs decided to expand into the suburban and urban business hotel product segment—can mitigate the risks.

Many in the industry believe, on balance, that the product or service expansion strategy is riskier than the market penetration strategy but roughly equal to the new geographic market strategy. However, companies may have little choice but to pursue this strategy from time to time, particularly after growth slows during the mature phase of the real estate cycle. In fact, whole product segments of a particular product type may become so overbuilt that the company must abandon its initial product or product segment. For example, the Linpro Company—a national firm that focused primarily on speculative commercial development but ran into trouble during the recession of the late 1980s and early 1990s—reinvented and repositioned itself as LCOR, a service provider that primarily did fee development for others, including the federal government. As the market for commercial speculative development has come back in the middle of the first decade of the 21st century, LCOR is returning to its roots, redeploying capital that was raised through its fee service businesses during the downturn into its original core business, capital-risk development projects.

New Business Strategy: New Product or Service, New Market

Entering a new metropolitan area to develop a new product or service type is the riskiest strategy a firm can follow. None of the firm's expertise, experience, and connections in its former market or product or service help it in its new endeavor. A change in both market and product factors can easily lead to failure, and achieving success requires great skill and many resources. Indeed, this is such a risky strategy that we can think of no examples of companies that have succeeded with it in recent years.

Several ways that a company can mitigate the risks of developing a new product type in a new market include building a product type that is similar to products the company has built in the past and entering into joint ventures with local companies. DMB Associates did both of those things when it began working with Rancho Mission Viejo in the late 1990s to build what became Ladera Ranch, one of the largest concentrations of "green" homes in the United States and the nation's largest solar community. Although DMB was an experienced community developer, its earlier projects had all been very high-end resort communities in Arizona and other resort locations. Ladera Ranch is a primary residential community in Orange County, California. To mitigate the risk of developing a new product type in a new geographic market, DMB entered a joint venture with a local partner, the landowner, that also had good development capabilities, was politically connected, and had a cadre of consultants and relationships with builders, so they could hit the ground running. Thus, DMB did not have to take all the market risk on its own.

Taking a company into a new metropolitan area to develop or service a new product segment within a known product type is only slightly less risky. An example is the convenience retail developer and manager in Atlanta that decided to enter the power center development and management business in Tampa, with only moderate success. This strategy should be carefully considered before it is pursued. Of course, many players in the industry assume that they are capable of any challenge, especially during the upturn or mature phases, when confidence—sometimes unfounded—runs high. The result, sometimes, is poor business decisions. At times, however, a company may have to adopt this growth strategy, particularly when a metropolitan area's economy goes into a steep recession and the demand for the company's products and services dries up even in other markets where demand for new segments is strong.

Rules of Engagement

At the same time that a company considers what it will do and for whom, it is important to address where the company will take on particular industry roles, and where it will not—in effect, its rules of engagement for taking on a particular industry role in a particular market. For example, the rules of engagement for a multifamily rental building developer and owner might entail finding markets with the characteristics shown in the box at right.

RULES OF ENGAGEMENT

- Strong job growth or household formation data
- High barriers to entry
- Non-union labor
- A location within one day's travel of the firm's core market
- The ability for the firm to own 500 to 1,500 units in the market within two to three years

Such a firm may decide to create different rules of engagement for different roles and thus might offer different products or services in different markets. For example, it may choose to provide construction or property management services to other firms for a fee in some markets but only to build and manage its own projects in others. The company also may decide to pursue some roles with certain products but not with others; for example, it may decide to construct its own stick-built garden products but to use third-party general contractors when it develops high rises.

Secondary Growth Strategies

A firm that is evaluating its strategy also should consider secondary growth strategies. These are extrapolated from the four basic strategies just outlined but demand greater attention because of their uniqueness.

The first secondary growth strategy is the development of a completely untried product type or product segment—in other words, investing in the research and testing of a heretofore unknown product or product segment in the hope not only of succeeding but also of getting a jump on the competition by rolling out the idea. Examples over the years have included extended-stay hotels, power town centers (a hybrid of town center and power center retail developments), condo hotels, and private residence clubs. Often, companies that innovate are able to experience rapid growth, at least for some period of time, until the market and competitors catch up.

Another secondary growth strategy is the development of an overseas business. Although this may not be part of every company's strategy, going global is just another dimension of the new market, same product or service strategy. Tishman Speyer is an example of a domestic company that made international market expansion a key part of its growth strategy. In 1988 Tishman became the first U.S. real estate company to develop and build a Class A office building in Germany. Nearly a decade later, the company broke ground in Brazil with a new Class A office building and recently formed a partnership to launch a building campaign in India. Tishman continues to leverage its vertical integration model; however, it uses the discipline imposed by its capital partners to select global markets.

Growth Strategies over Time

The ideal growth strategy evolves over time (figure 6-3). A company starts by maximizing the penetration of its current market with existing products and services. As that strategy matures, the company seeks to expand its product, product segment, and service offerings, while simultaneously or sequentially expanding into new markets to execute products and services within its area of expertise. As the company develops expertise with new products, segments, or services in its expanded market portfolio, it continues to export that new product, segment, and service expertise to other portfolio markets, as well as expand into new markets with these now well-developed offerings. Before long, the company is engaged in

Figure 6-3: GROWTH STRATEGIES OVER TIME

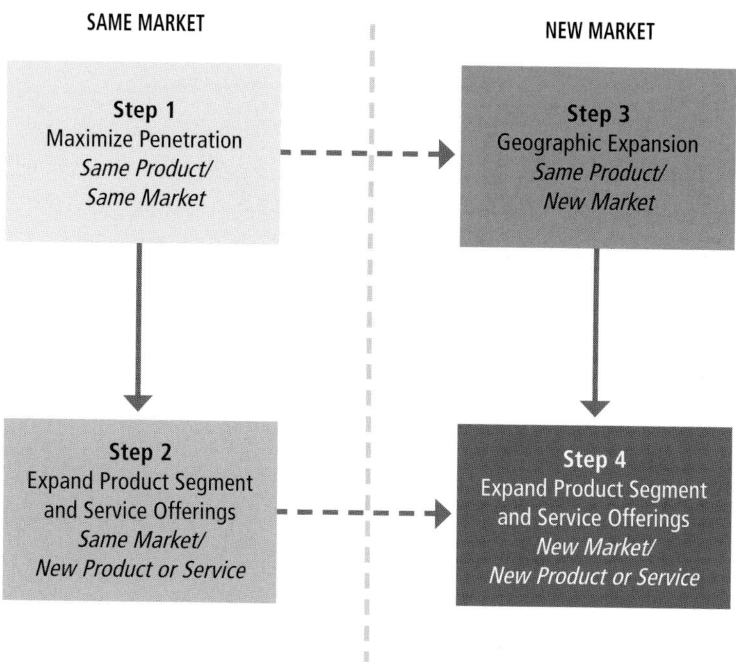

new products and in new markets relative to where it started, but it has made the move carefully, incrementally, and in a measured way.

Joseph Freed and Associates LLC, a Chicago-based developer, is a good example of a company that has followed this evolutionary growth strategy pattern. In 1965, the company started with a focus on retail in the greater Chicago metropolitan region. In the late 1980s, Freed was looking for additional growth opportunities and made a strategic move to diversify its product mix in its home market, to other commercial and residential segments. Leveraging the company's reputation and success in retail to other product types, Freed's development activities grew rapidly to include residential, office, mixed-use, and urban infill. Soon, the company developed strong expertise in mixed-use development (featuring retail, residential, office, and restaurant uses), and became recognized for its quality projects in Chicago.

In the late 1990s, the company's leaders—still eager for more growth opportunities and concerned that they were overly dependent on one market—entered the next stage of growth and embarked on a geographic market expansion strategy outside the company's core Chicago market. The first steps were small ones, concentrating on mixed-use commercial and residential projects in Detroit and Ann Arbor, Michigan. Soon thereafter, the company began to take longer strides away from the Midwest, most recently in Las Vegas, Denver, and North Carolina.

Setting Metrics

Before embarking on market, product, or service expansion strategies, a firm should prepare detailed business plans. The plans should specify the rules of engagement for these strategies, by articulating the company's business activity goals and objectives, threshold return expectations, time frames, accountability, and metrics for measuring progress toward the objectives. For example, a company growth strategy that says "We're going to grow our business by improving our market penetration of retail space in the Seattle market" must first define the company's current position in that market and where it expects—or hopes—to be in five, six, or ten years. It also must include benchmarks that the company can use to monitor its progress toward achieving those goals. The company certainly may revisit and revise those goals as time goes by, but it must have goals and a means to measure its progress toward them. These metrics should help the firm determine whether or not its strategies are succeeding.

Company executives might begin the geographic deployment strategy process by simply saying, "We're going to expand our markets. As we sit here today, we don't know which markets offer the best opportunities, but we know that we need to diversify and grow outside of our core market. As we go about looking for opportunities to do so, we're going to look for opportunities in markets that have the following characteristics." Setting the rules of engagement in this way, defining the "corral" of opportunities that the company will pursue, helps guide the employees farther down the chain of command who are tasked with identifying these opportunities and markets. Company leaders may say, for example, "We need to identify markets in which we can be sure we can grow to a certain sustainable size over a three- to five-year period"—or develop a certain number of office buildings or apartment complexes within a similar time frame—"in order to support a full-service team of developers and property managers." This statement helps company employees identify the markets in which they should be pursuing deals and, likewise, lets them know that they should avoid doing one-off deals in other markets, because those deals would pull the company off the strategic path of gaining market share and hinder the organizational efficiency and effectiveness that comes from having a certain presence in the market.

Fore Property Company, a national developer and manager of multifamily housing projects, found itself with a lot of "onesies and twosies": projects that were spread all over the country, without a sufficient concentration to enable the company to operate and manage them efficiently or effectively. As part of their strategy planning process, Fore's leaders began to define the criteria that they would use to decide which markets they would go into (and which they would pull out of), from an efficiency standpoint. They made a conscious decision to focus on markets in which the company could support a full-service development, construction, and operations team within a three-year time frame.

Companies also may set financial metrics—including risk-adjusted return criteria—to help determine when and where to enter a new market or product type, or to expand their presence in an existing market. When Paradigm Properties, which began as a developer and operator of student apartments in Gainesville, Florida, decided to grow beyond its core Florida markets and expand into conventional apartments in other cities and states, it set up a variety of financial metrics that were dependent on product type and a project's distance from Paradigm's core operations. The company has a much lower rate-of-return hurdle for a student housing project in Gainesville—one that is a simple addition to its portfolio—than it has for a conventional apartment project in a new market, from which it would expect much higher returns to offset the risk of entering that new market. Paradigm's executives have held to the discipline provided by these metrics when determining which projects to execute.

These types of market position strategies will be discussed in more detail in the following chapter. What is important to recognize here is that, regardless of the strategy, companies should develop benchmarks and other metrics to inform and measure the success of their growth and geographic deployment strategies.

CHAPTER 7

Profitability Strategies

Profitability strategies are focused on ways to improve efficiency and profitability, both to optimize top-line revenues and to get more top-line revenues to drop to the bottom line while maintaining—or improving—quality. This includes methods that reduce the cost of doing business, increase the speed at which the company delivers products or services, and improve customer satisfaction.

Profitability strategies are given much more attention as a company reaches the end of the mature phase of the real estate cycle and growth strategies become much less important. These strategies should be pursued aggressively in preparation for a downturn; they are central to improving profit margins and offsetting the slowdown in growth. Most companies tend to address profitability later, usually after the cycle has shifted.

Strategies that improve a company's efficiency have both direct and indirect impacts on profitability. Just as with growth strategies, any company seeking to improve its efficiency should first determine how it will establish benchmarks and measure improvements in efficiency. It should evaluate the appropriate level of staff and overhead for various functions and should commit to achieving continuous improvements in cost reduction and efficiency. When setting goals and benchmarks, it is critical to determine who the "customers" are for the services performed by each group within the company (see chapter 6), in which areas or by which methods cost reduction and efficiency improvements can be made most effectively, and how efficiency improvements will be tied to the company's compensation plan (see chapter 8).

Wherever possible, a company should strive to define benchmarks and measures in absolute and relative (to peer group) terms. However, where relative data are difficult or expensive to gather—or are suspect, owing to variations in accounting methods, comparability of peer group, and so forth—companies should measure efficiency gains against internal benchmarks only. To maximize efficiency in its profitability strategy, a firm should make a conscious effort to use information that is already being generated in the organization and not get trapped in an "analysis-paralysis doom loop." In other words, the company should avoid becoming distracted from the important work of executing its core strategy just to generate a bunch of new metrics. It must find the right balance; it needs enough information to evaluate progress but not too much information, which can paralyze effective decision making.

Growing the Top Line

One major profitability strategy that executives often overlook is growing the top line. A company's top managers should challenge themselves constantly to make sure that they are, in fact, charging as much as they can for products and services. First, they should be sure they understand where, historically, they have made money. Then they should examine whether they have optimized their top-line revenue numbers. Increasing profits does not just mean growing by adding new buildings or new residential units; it also should involve maximizing the income that a company is getting from its existing properties and services. This strategy thus involves ensuring that the company is optimizing its revenue stream. Doing so requires a clear understanding of the firm's competitive positioning in a marketplace, as well as knowledge about what the company's competitors are doing.

Going back to the issues of customer strategy and core competencies, what do the company's customers value in its products, services, and—let us not forget—brand? Is the company truly capturing all the value that it is delivering to its customers? A company may be able to leverage its existing customer base to get customers to spend more time and more money with the firm for different but related types of services. While selling through ancillary services may not be a sure path to growing revenues exponentially, as some in the rental apartment business were predicting in the mid-1990s, it can still make a meaningful contribution to a company's profitability. Every opportunity should be explored and at least considered.

With that said, a company also should carefully analyze whether it should get into the web portal, insurance, telecommunications, title, and insurance businesses or whether it would make more sense to partner with established providers of these services and accept a share of the revenues or the profits in return. Companies that spend too much time building ancillary services run the risk of taking their focus off their core business or customer.

Occasionally, companies discover "found" money by changing business practices. For example, rental apartment operators in the 1990s who were faced with increasing utility bills found that by submetering water they could shift the cost of this utility onto residents, without any offsetting decrease in rents. Other operators have become creative by charging residents one-time amenity fees or key charges as a way to boost revenues without doing anything more or different than they had in the past.

Other Profitability Strategies

A number of other strategies can help companies improve profitability and get more top-line revenues to drop to the bottom line (see feature box). They are described in the following subsections.

OTHER PROFITABILITY STRATEGIES

1. Technology and systems
2. Outsourcing and offshoring
3. Product standardization
4. Supply improvement strategy
5. Traditional cost cutting
6. Cycle time
7. Customer satisfaction
8. Market position

Technology and Systems

Although not a strategy itself, technology—including information and communication systems—is a powerful tool to facilitate increases in efficiency and effectiveness. It is often an important element in a firm's profitability strategies. Investments in technology that enable a company to enhance communication, provide better and more timely information, and automate time-consuming processes can reduce overhead costs and increase efficiency throughout the organization.

During the past several decades, the real estate industry has taken huge strides in improving efficiencies through the use of sophisticated, state-of-the-art technology. Uses range from property and market databases to Internet-based property listing services, from wireless communications systems that allow property management staff to track and manage maintenance requests, costs, and scheduling to those that provide financial managers with up-to-date information and allow them to record, report, and archive financial transactions. Similarly, information about real estate markets and product trends is increasingly available and affordable. This increased transparency has improved companies' ability to make informed decisions about investments, but tremendous inefficiencies in the marketplace still create challenges—and opportunities—for real estate companies.

Real estate companies are increasingly tapping tools and techniques from other industries and applying them to real estate. Archstone-Smith, for example, uses a pricing model borrowed from the travel industry to adjust its apartment rents in real time, in response to changes in the company's occupancy and revenues as well as market supply and demand conditions. Crescent Resources has been using sophisticated financial instruments, such as shorting stocks of homebuilders, as a hedge to minimize risk in its land development activities. AvalonBay brought on a senior-level marketing executive with experience in brand management in the tobacco and consumer products industries to help lead its branding efforts.

Outsourcing and Offshoring

Another way to improve a company's profitability and efficiency is to outsource, taking some service business roles out of house by subcontracting them to local, regional, national, or even international (offshore) operators. Companies that are exploring this option must decide which services to subcontract and which to perform in house. This is the classic "buy versus make" decision that all businesses—not only real estate companies—face daily. The decision should be based not only on cost but also on control, quality, top management preferences, expertise and creativity, and the desire for business service income. These issues are discussed in more detail below.

Cost. If the success of a service business depends on economies of scale or involves a significant learning curve, the company generally finds it cost-effective to subcontract its service. Most real estate service businesses, however, require experienced staff in order to perform their work cost-effectively. Therefore, the decision usually is a matter of whether the firm has a sufficient amount of work to keep the required minimum number of skilled in-house personnel busy full time.

When it comes to such functions as architecture, planning, market analysis, and others that are not among a company's core competencies yet are disciplines in which it recognizes that it needs best-of-class services, many companies make a conscious decision not to internalize these processes. Instead, they assemble teams of top-quality, leading firms to attack specific projects as needed.

Traditionally, multifamily companies have had internal property management operations. As the price of those services dropped, as the quality of third-party management increased, and as the investment required to maintain state-of-the-art status increased (from the perspective of both technology and human capital), more and more apartment companies have been outsourcing their property management operations. The companies that have decided to pay a third-party provider a fee for these services have been able to reduce their headaches—as well as their payroll and other costs—while still providing high-quality service to their tenants. Owners of relatively small portfolios of office and retail properties also are finding themselves in this situation. Maintaining internal property management functions can be a burden for companies that are not large enough to justify a fixed investment in an in-house operation.

Control. Maintaining maximum control over performance, which is essential to the creation or maintenance of value in fields such as marketing or management, is the primary reason for performing a service in house. There are numerous examples of multifamily developers or owners that have been unwilling to part with their in-house property management service. In many instances, the company's leaders recognize that they may not have the most efficient property management operation—in fact, some admit freely that they are overpaying for their internal property management services. Still, they made a conscious decision to retain property management in house because, as long-term property holders, they believe that this is the best way to achieve their ultimate goal of preserving and growing value in the portfolio over the long run. This consideration outweighs any short-term "overpayment" on property management.

Quality. An outside contractor may be able to maintain higher quality than an in-house department because the service is the contractor's full-time focus. For the real estate company, quality control may be only a part-time job in some aspects of the development process. Some developers with in-house general contracting capabilities occasionally bid out construction jobs to third-party providers, just to stay in touch with market pricing and keep their in-house function sharp.

Top Management Preferences. The top managers of a firm often have no interest in providing a particular service and therefore prefer to subcontract it. Property management is typically one of the functions about which company leaders have strong preferences. One camp views this function as a key element in its ability to lease-up and stabilize development projects and to maintain long-term value. Most REITs manage their own properties, as a key part of their "story." The other camp views property management, particularly third-party property management, as a low-margin, management-intensive business that often is a cost center, not a profit center.

In 2005, Trammell Crow Residential—which had been in the first camp for many years—sold its in-house property management division to its senior partners. It had determined that the company's management capital was better spent on higher-value activities such as investment building of apartment communities. The leaders of the company recognized that there was an opportunity cost to being in rental property management. The top managers had to spend time on that relatively low-value activity instead of concentrating on what made the most money for them, which was the high value-added industry role of developing new apartments. Other executives are well advised to consider the opportunity costs involved in performing ancillary service businesses in house, when they are evaluating existing or potential businesses or activities.

Product Standardization

For companies that take on capital risk roles such as building development, product standardization increases the standardization of designs, components, and construction processes. Standardization can easily lead to lower construction costs, improved quality, and increased profits. It particularly benefits those firms that have adopted either the market expansion strategy or the market penetration strategy, both of which may lend themselves to cookie-cutter projects.

Hotels, fast-food outlets, and big-box retail stores are among the best examples of product standardization.

Except in very rare occasions, the standard Hilton Garden Inn prototype dictates whether a particular site will work, as opposed to the other way around, in which the configuration of a project is modified to conform to the site. Big-box retailers are becoming more creative with their store configurations as they seek growth opportunities in supply-constrained markets and increasingly seek infill and more urban locations—but suburban Super Wal-Mart, Costco, and Home Depot stores look virtually identical across the country.

As more real estate companies standardize their products, some may question whether they are still in the real estate industry. The experience of the restaurant and hotel sectors is instructive. As restaurant and hotel developers standardized their products during the past 40 years, they left the real estate industry and created entirely new businesses. These companies are now almost exclusively in the service, management, and franchise sectors. They lay off development risk and, in many cases, even the ownership of the real estate on partners and investors.

Supply Improvement Strategy

The supply improvement strategy focuses company attention on lowering costs and increasing reliability in the delivery of the components or services needed to produce a company's product. Supplies include standard building components (such as heating, ventilating, and air conditioning systems, elevators, and plumbing), financing, and architectural services. For capital risk players, supply improvement applies to finance, construction, land, and the vast number of services needed in the development process. For service business providers, supply improvement applies to vendors and subcontractors who are part of the support base for the service. Through bulk purchasing and regional or national contracts, large firms are able to leverage their size to reduce the cost of supplies, thus increasing their efficiency.

The supply improvement strategy also helps a company achieve high quality and customer satisfaction. Thus, it is crucial to engage the cooperation of and coordinate efforts with component and service providers. Obtaining the cooperation of vendors is hard to do; the process must be managed constantly to maintain good relationships.

Traditional Cost Cutting

When costs must be reduced quickly and management does not have time to analyze operations department by department or function by function, a company may turn to traditional cost cutting. Reducing costs by a certain percentage across the board is a crude means of obtaining efficiency. Its effects generally are difficult to predict; however, it can prove useful if all other attempts at cost containment have been tried and top managers still need to reduce costs.

For example, a large income property firm in the Southeast had an obviously bloated annual overhead of $12 million. After trying to reduce costs and improve efficiencies in selected departments, the president became frustrated and demanded that every department cut costs by 20 percent. After the cuts—which were mainly in personnel—the company seemed to function much the same as it had previously, prompting management to ask how many more cuts could be made before efficient operations were affected.

Cycle Time

Cycle time refers to how long it takes to build something; it is a particularly important element of profitability for homebuilders, although most real estate sectors are sensitive to the time it takes to deliver and stabilize a project. Many homebuilders, both national and regional, are focusing on reducing the amount of time it takes to deliver a unit. By shaving just three or four days off the average time, a company can gain significant savings in interest carrying costs alone and can improve the turnover of capital, another important measure of profitability. If a homebuilder can achieve a 10 percent margin but can harvest and reinvest its equity capital once every three months rather than once every four months, it will make a significant impact on the annual return on capital. A number of companies therefore have set targets, aiming to reduce their cycle time from, say, 120 days to 90 days over some period of time. Everyone in the development business—not only homebuilders—should consider cycle time and be cognizant of the old adage that "time is money."

Customer Satisfaction

Attracting new residents, tenants, or other types of customers to replace those who leave can be quite expensive, so another very astute profitability strategy involves reducing customer turnover. The best way to retain customers is to keep them happy. Office tenants who believe that their building is the best in the area—with the best location, the best service, or the best customer-oriented experience for the value—are less likely to leave than those who are unhappy. They are more likely to convince their friends and associates to relocate to the building and to lease additional space in it as their own businesses expand. Likewise, happy apartment residents are more likely to tell their friends, "Hey, you've got to live in this place—it has everything you need, the rent is reasonable, and the service is great." To the extent that companies avoid having to market space (by reducing turnover) and can rely on word of mouth and referrals to do their marketing, as opposed to spending large sums of money advertising, they can reap huge benefits from customer satisfaction.

Market Position

Another way for a company to improve efficiency and profitability involves establishing a particular level of market position or penetration in its chosen markets or submarkets. Market positioning is about identifying the markets and locations in which a company can gain sufficient foothold so that, at a minimum, it can gain operational efficiencies. Taking this strategy a step further, real estate companies may aim to grow their market share in ways that begin to afford them significant economies of scale and pricing power.

A company's market position can range from market presence (the minimum existence in a market necessary to gain operational efficiencies) to market recognition (when a company can not only support a full-service team but also begin to enjoy significant economies of scale) to market dominance (when a company enjoys all the benefits of scale and also can begin to influence pricing to its advantage). As an example, figure 7-1 outlines key metrics that many companies in the industry believe are valid for various market positions in the rental apartment segment.

Figure 7-1: MARKET POSITION METRICS FOR RENTAL APARTMENTS

POSITION	SHARE (%)	UNITS (#)	EFFICIENCY
Market Presence	3%	600–1,500	Management
Market Recognition	10%	2,000–4,000	Expense
Market Dominance	>30%	5,000–10,000	Revenue

The time frame necessary to achieve the desired position depends on a wide range of external and internal factors. The availability of human resources and operating systems are among the internal considerations, while market prices, the competitive landscape, and the availability of capital are among the external ones.

Market Presence. Market presence is defined as owning or operating the minimum critical mass of projects or units in a given market or markets necessary to achieve management efficiencies in each market. For many apartment operators, this translates into a minimum of three properties with at least 600 apartment homes within a one-hour driving radius of each other. This efficiency measure often is used to guide a company's growth and geographic deployment strategy: a company will choose to pursue opportunities in markets or submarkets that it believes it can enter and in which it believes it can maintain at least a market presence status. Disciplined companies that cannot—or do not want to—achieve at least a market presence in the medium term often make the strategic decision to get out of that market, subject to market timing.

Market Recognition. Once a company has achieved market presence in one or more markets, it may strive to achieve market recognition status in some or all of these markets. "Market recognition status" is defined as a substantial presence that enables a company to achieve brand recognition as well as marketing and operational efficiencies. This status also enables the company to achieve additional management and expense efficiencies and the marketing advantages associated with brand recognition. Some of those advantages for real estate companies include the ability to retain relocating tenants, lower turnover rates, lower ongoing marketing costs (including the ability to sell multiple properties in a single advertisement), and—possibly—higher rents. Successful branding typically requires a critical mass of product or services in a market area, a product or service that can be clearly differentiated from the competition, the ability to maintain consistent quality, a significant investment in the brand, and—finally—patience.

Market Dominance. In the long term, a firm may chose to pursue a market dominance strategy in selected submarkets, where it may be able to enjoy a pricing advantage by dominating a submarket. Dominance is likely to be a long-term strategy, because it typically requires capturing at least one-third—and sometimes more than half—of a certain grade or quality of assets within the defined submarket. Whether a single company has the ability to affect rents through market recognition or domination is controversial. Although some analysts believe that a firm can do it with 20 percent to 50 percent of the units or space in a submarket, others do not believe that a single company can affect rents. Still others contend that dominating a metropolitan area market is so difficult that the only way to do so is with massive assets, such as a concentration of regional malls.

A company that is interested in increasing its efficiency and profitability by increasing its market penetration should develop a prioritization plan for the markets in which it currently operates (and those to which it plans to expand), setting a targeted level of market penetration, a time frame for accomplishing this level of penetration, and a method (for example, development or acquisition) by which the target will be reached.

Although the market dominance theory may not apply to all areas of the real estate industry, many firms believe that both marketing and management economies of scale emerge as a company achieves a greater market share, resulting in higher profits. In marketing, for example, almost all new build-to-suit, leasing, management, and development deals seek out the dominant player to obtain a bid or proposal. From a management point of view, dominance may result in the physical proximity of projects, which can reduce travel time and costs for supervisors and maintenance personnel.

The Final Word

Profitability strategies tend not to receive much attention in the real estate industry. They are certainly not as exciting as the industry role and growth strategies discussed in preceding chapters, but they will play a vital role in the first decade of the 21st century and beyond, as the industry becomes increasingly institutionally oriented and sophisticated.

CHAPTER 8

Organizational Strategies

Organizational strategies pertain to designing an organizational structure that best allows a company to fulfill its mission and achieve its goals. In short, they are how a company organizes itself to execute its business. Real estate companies can choose from two basic organizational structures: process oriented or project oriented. However, most companies typically use a hybrid of the two or a matrix organization. Real estate companies that have multiple divisions or offices also need to address the issue of centralization and decentralization.

There is no right or wrong structure; the challenge is to determine which approach or combination of approaches works best for a given company. Each strategy raises a multitude of issues for consideration. Which combination of process and project orientation is right for the firm? How centralized or decentralized should the firm's structure be? To what extent should a company have redundant capabilities, and where can it leverage shared resources? Once a company has defined its ideal or optimal structure, it needs to map out a plan for transitioning from where it is today to where it wants to be in its ultimate end state.

Another important organizational issue involves succession planning—that is, planning the grooming and training of the next generation of leaders—and for the planned, or possibly unexpected, departure of a firm's senior managers. At General Electric, part of every senior manager's job description is planning for and training one's own replacement. Every company that seeks to create a sustainable organization needs to put in place and maintain a succession plan for each key senior staff position, whether that involves grooming and promoting people from within the organization or hiring them from outside. Have senior managers thought about how the company will continue to function after they leave? A chief financial officer or managing director may be hit by a bus tomorrow, or he or she may be planning to retire in five years; sustainable organizations must be prepared for either event.

Compensation is yet another important organizational issue. Every real estate company should ensure that its compensation plan dovetails with and supports the strategic plan. As with organizational structures, there are many types of compensation plans and no one formula works for all organizations. Each company must tailor its compensation system to its strategy, structure, and personality. Most important, the company must devise a compensation program that aligns the interests of the executive team and the rest of the organization with the company's strategic objectives. As it does so, the company should consider several factors, including striking the right balance between fixed compensation (base salaries) and variable compensation (bonuses, long-term incentives, and so forth), the extent to which the compensation system is linked to quantitative and qualitative factors, and the extent to which the system is split between individual performance and corporate performance.

Real estate companies also must deal with growth and organizational expansion (or contraction) issues that are specific to each phase of the real estate cycle. During the upturn phase, management must determine how to structure and staff a growing organization. For example, when expanding into new markets, should the firm move senior managers from one location to another or hire a new manager who already knows the new market? (There are pros and cons to both options.) During the mature phase, the firm must recognize that some of the greatest potential for profit improvement comes with the greater efficiency that is born of improved organizational strategies. During a downturn, management must address, among other matters, the redefinition of job descriptions, under- and overcapacity problems and—perhaps most important—morale problems caused by the organization's potential shrinkage. Often in a downturn, a firm must wrestle with how to achieve a balance between maintaining its core capabilities so that it can prosper when the market improves and right-sizing its overhead to suit its current income.

Organizational Structure and Character

A real estate company faces a spectrum of organizational structure options. On one side is the process-oriented or functional structure. On the other is the project-oriented or project management structure. These should be viewed as two bookends; the organizational structures of most real estate companies lie between them, combining aspects of both structures.

When a company selects a process-oriented structure, each step of its business is handled by specialists. As the specialists complete their parts of the process, other specialists take over. The best analogy for a process-oriented operation is a relay team running a race: each member of the team does his or her part and then passes the baton to the next runner. In contrast, the project-oriented structure revolves around a generalist who supervises all functions necessary to complete the project or deliver the service. In a company with a project-oriented structure, a single individual takes responsibility for all aspects of a project from cradle to grave, including, for example, site acquisition, entitlement, financing, construction, stabilization, and possibly eventual disposition. The analogy here is a triathlete who swims, bikes, and runs.

Process Orientation

The process orientation involves a series of handoffs from one specialist or department to another. A process-oriented organization employs functional specialists, each of whom is responsible for a segment of the process. For example, it employs specialists in site acquisition, entitlements, land development, construction, marketing, leasing, property management, and asset management. Process-oriented service businesses employ specialists to market the service, others to perform the service, and still others to report on the performance of the service. Each specialist performs his or her assigned job for each new project that comes through the company or for each new client, handing it off upon completion to the next specialist in line.

Looking at the development of a typical rental apartment project, for example, in a pure process-oriented company, one person (or department) is responsible for identifying potential development sites. After identifying a prospective site, that person hands off the project to someone else, who takes responsibility for getting the project planned, designed, entitled, and approved. That person then turns it over to someone who is responsible for getting the project financed, and in some cases presold, and then on to someone who gets the apartment building or complex built. That person then passes the project on to someone who is responsible for getting it leased-up and stabilized, who in turn hands it over to someone who, possibly, will manage it over the long term. Many single-purpose real estate companies, particularly REITs, are set up in this way.

The process-oriented structure tends to work particularly well for cookie-cutter products, those that can be repeated easily with only minor differences. A Marriott Residence Inn, for example, is a well-defined product; it needs to be built on a site with a particular set of requirements, and the buildings and financing structures tend to be quite similar. Therefore, it is relatively easy for one person to find a group of potential sites that meet the necessary criteria, then hand them off to the person who is responsible for doing the financial feasibility testing for each site, and so forth through the process.

The advantage of the process-oriented structure is that the firm can devote a high level of skill to each step. The major disadvantage is that this structure needs a certain volume or a certain number of projects or clients in the pipeline in order to keep the organization operating at full capacity. Those projects, moreover, need to be distributed evenly to prevent an overload of work in one department while specialists in other departments remain temporarily idle. Another downside stems from the simple fact that the process by its nature involves a series of handoffs, and every time a handoff occurs there can be an "oops" moment in which the "baton" is dropped. With this structure, typically no single person is responsible for seeing a project through from cradle to grave.

Project Orientation

At the other end of the spectrum is the project orientation. With this structure, a single individual—or team—is responsible for seeing a project through from start to finish. At a project-oriented company that develops office buildings, for example, a project manager is involved in finding a site for a new project, getting it entitled, working out the capitalization, and overseeing the construction, marketing, and leasing processes, and possibly the sale of the project. Although that person or team may pull in other resources from other parts of the company, he or she is responsible for the project's ultimate success or failure.

One example of a project-oriented company is Trammell Crow Residential, which has 15 local divisions. The president of each division—its senior managing director—oversees everything that division does. Below each senior managing director are managing directors—who also are partners—who typically oversee two or three projects at a time. Although the company has several land acquisition experts in southern California, for most projects the managing directors find the sites, get the projects designed, and take them all the way through the development process. Finance is decentralized to the division level, although the divisions receive some help from the company's chief financial officer. Construction typically is done locally; Trammell Crow Residential has about 11 construction companies, several of which do work for more than one division.

The project-oriented structure works particularly well for companies that tend to have complex or one-of-a-kind projects with complicated real estate questions and issues, because in those types of projects the opportunities for something to go wrong in a handoff are great and extremely costly. When a company is developing an urban mixed-use project, or a suburban multiuse project that blends rental apartments with for-sale townhouses and retail space, or any other type of project that is different and, in some sense, unique—the type of project that may never have been done before or may never be done again—a single person or team is needed to keep very tight control of every aspect of the project, simply because it is so complicated and there is no manual to tell a specialist how to do it.

Other primary advantages of the project-oriented structure are its modular nature and the clarity of responsibility and authority. That is, the organization does not need several projects in the pipeline to keep it operating efficiently, and there is never any doubt about who is in charge. The minimum amount of business is the amount necessary to keep one person busy. The major disadvantage, clearly, is that this structure requires expertise in multiple dimensions, something hard to find in any one individual or small team. A good development project manager or executive must understand all aspects of the development process, from the market to entitlements to construction, marketing, and leasing—the whole package. It is rare to find one person who commands all the skills required to complete a project or deliver a service successfully. Therefore, supplemental skills often need to be provided at some level in the company. For example, a project manager who came up through the construction side of the business may need help with finance, marketing, or leasing. For these reasons many real estate companies choose the hybrid organization structure, which will be discussed further.

Project Process Characteristics

Project-oriented and process-oriented operations often demand markedly different marketing, financial, and organizational skills (figure 8-1). From a marketing perspective, each aspect of a project-oriented business is one of a kind. The efficiency associated with any given project is extremely low because little can be replicated from one deal to the next. Each new real estate development or new acquisition or repositioning project has unique characteristics in terms of its legal structure, financial structure, architecture, and overall challenges. One of the best examples of a project-oriented business is filmmaking, the industry that coined the expression "You're only as good as your last picture." In real estate development, most project-oriented players are only as good as their last project.

In contrast, process-oriented service businesses are characterized by a continuous flow of repeat customers or by different customers whose needs are similar to those of past customers. An example of an outstanding process-oriented company is McDonald's, whose motto is "Billions and billions served"—that is, identical hamburgers purchased by both new and repeat customers.

Financing a project-oriented business is by necessity a constant challenge. Most process-oriented businesses, by contrast, have a relatively stable cash flow and customer base. Consequently, their financial structure is more uniform. The

Figure 8-1: MARKETING CHARACTERISTICS

PROJECT ORIENTED	PROCESS ORIENTED
• One project at a time • No guarantee of next project • Each project generally has different characteristics and structure • Higher margins • Higher risk	• Continuous stream of business • Repeat business generally ensured if customers are satisfied • Customers are more likely to be similar • Lower margins (although there are exceptions) • Lower risk

Figure 8-2: FINANCIAL CHARACTERISTICS

PROJECT ORIENTED

- Unique deal structure
- Constantly changing financing markets for both equity and debt
- Project-by-project financing
- Significant financing needs for the project to proceed
- Limited access to public equity markets
- Potential for major surprises, requiring constant restructuring of financing vehicles

PROCESS ORIENTED

- More uniform contract structure
- More consistent financing
- Corporate or entity-level financing more readily available
- Less financial structuring required, in some cases only working capital needed
- Broader access to public equity markets
- More stable financing structure

capital that process-oriented businesses need is much less than the amounts that project-oriented firms need for capital risk development and acquisitions (figure 8-2). Process-oriented businesses usually require working capital of about 12 percent to 25 percent of annual sales volume in order to cover outstanding accounts receivable and other day-to-day financing needs. Thus, the stability of the cash flow is well suited to conventional bank financing and, potentially, can mean access to the public equity market.

In terms of organizational structure, the project-oriented business can look more like a job shop, bursting with barely contained anarchy, excitement, burnout, and high turnover. By contrast, the process-oriented business often resembles an assembly line or an efficient organization with a more stable workforce (figure 8-3).

Figure 8-3: ORGANIZATIONAL CHARACTERISTICS

PROJECT ORIENTED

- Job shop
- Chaotic, exciting, stressful, and constantly changing
- Fighter pilots
- High turnover
- Addicted to change

PROCESS ORIENTED

- Assembly line
- Consistent, orderly
- Bomber pilots
- More stable workforce
- Slower adjustments to change

Matrix or Hybrid

As mentioned above, most real estate companies, particularly those in the development and building segments of the business, are not purely project or process oriented but rather some mix of the two. They have adopted a hybrid or matrix organizational structure. Many real estate development companies, particularly those working on unique, one-off development projects, adopt a predominantly project-oriented structure, with various process or functional overlays to support their project managers. In these matrix organizations, a project manager is responsible for a given development from start to finish but can draw upon centralized corporate resources for discrete tasks. Common functional groups typically include such areas as financing and capital markets, construction, marketing and sales, leasing, and property management.

There is no right or wrong answer to the question of how an organization should structure itself. The skills and interests of the company's managers should guide and inform the appropriate structure. If top managers have financial talent, for example, they usually keep that function specialized. The structural decision also is based on their company philosophy. If the top managers want to control particular aspects of the business process, they will tend to develop a more process-oriented organizational structure. If the management philosophy favors delegation to the maximum extent possible, the company's structure will tend to be more project oriented.

Centralized versus Decentralized

Companies with multiple product types, divisions, or geographic markets typically also must identify how centralized or decentralized the organizational structure should be. For example, if a process-oriented developer of industrial space is active in several markets, it needs to identify to what extent each geographic region should have independent and redundant capabilities in, say, entitlement, finance, construction, leasing, and management. Should each division mirror every other division, with similar capabilities, or should some companywide capabilities be centrally located and made available as a resource to all the company's regions or divisions?

Decentralized companies allow individual divisions or offices in multiple locations to operate with a great deal of autonomy; divisions or branch offices may be set up as mirror images of the home office, independent satellites that operate without much oversight or input from headquarters (figure 8-4). A decentralized construction management company, for example, might maintain full-service teams with development, construction, and management capabilities in each of its branch offices, so that each team can operate independently. While these teams might share a company name, history, capital sources, and so forth, they are essentially independent operators.

At the opposite end of the spectrum, centralized companies maintain most of the capabilities for executing their business within a central division or headquarters office. The centralized construction management company may have individual developers (or development teams) working out of branch offices, but it will require them to use the firm's centralized construction, financing, and property management functions. By keeping these functions centralized, the company can maintain economies of scale, consistency, and quality control.

Functions such as human resources, information technology, legal affairs, risk analysis, management, and insurance are typically centralized, as is financing, although some companies that operate in multiple locations allow each local office to obtain its own financing (figure 8-5). A number of multimarket companies have a decentralized financing function: capital is generated locally, but a centralized corporate investment committee must approve all deals.

As with the project or process orientation, many companies adopt a matrix organizational structure when it comes to centralization or decentralization (figure 8-6). The most common choice for companies that operate in multiple markets tends to be a decentralized regional structure. Each region is largely autonomous, responsible for sourcing and executing its own deals and accountable for its own profit and loss, but with centralized functional overlays, such as accounting, human resources, information technology, treasury, and risk management.

Succession Planning

A company must consider how to put in place and maintain a plan to grow or groom the next generation of leaders. It should be in a position to replace senior managers without disrupting the business in the event of either expected turnover, such as an executive's retirement, or unexpected turnover, such as a manager's sudden death or departure to work for another firm. Often, the impending departure or unexpected turnover triggers a strategic planning process:

Figure 8-4: DECENTRALIZED ORGANIZATIONAL STRUCTURE

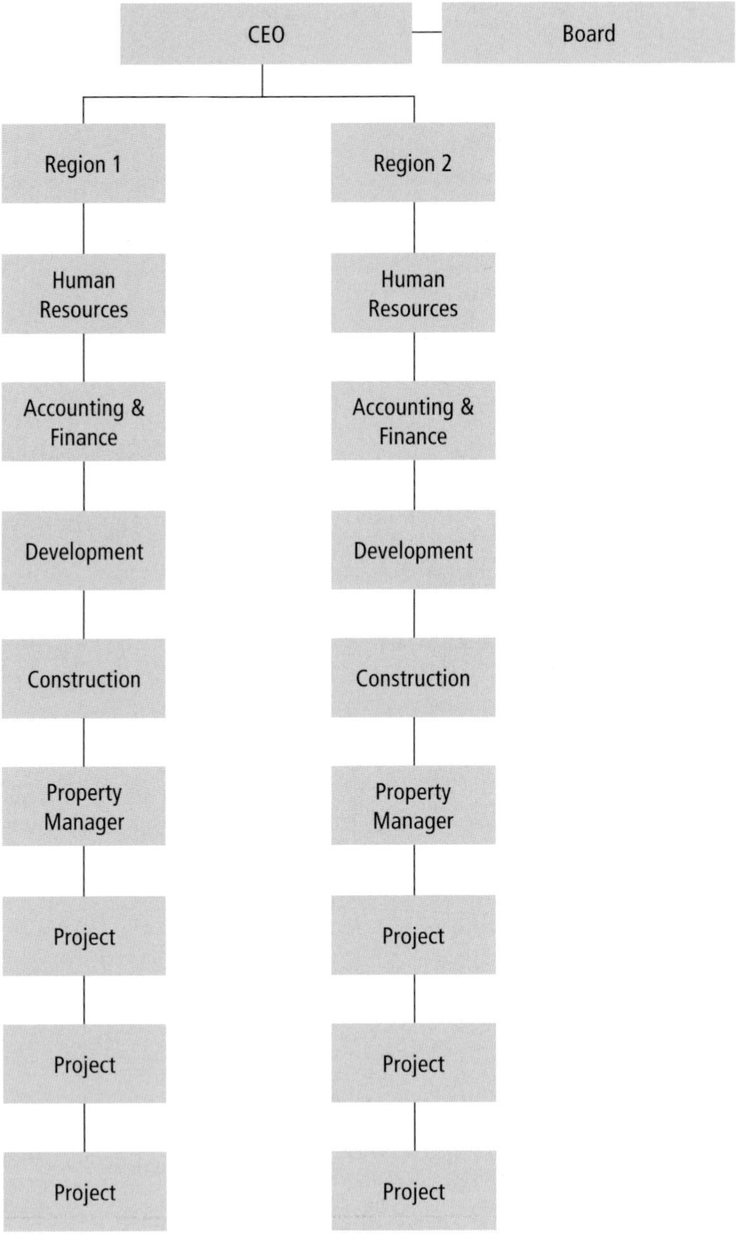

CEO — Board

Region 1	Region 2
Human Resources	Human Resources
Accounting & Finance	Accounting & Finance
Development	Development
Construction	Construction
Property Manager	Property Manager
Project	Project
Project	Project
Project	Project

Figure 8-5: CENTRALIZED ORGANIZATIONAL STRUCTURE

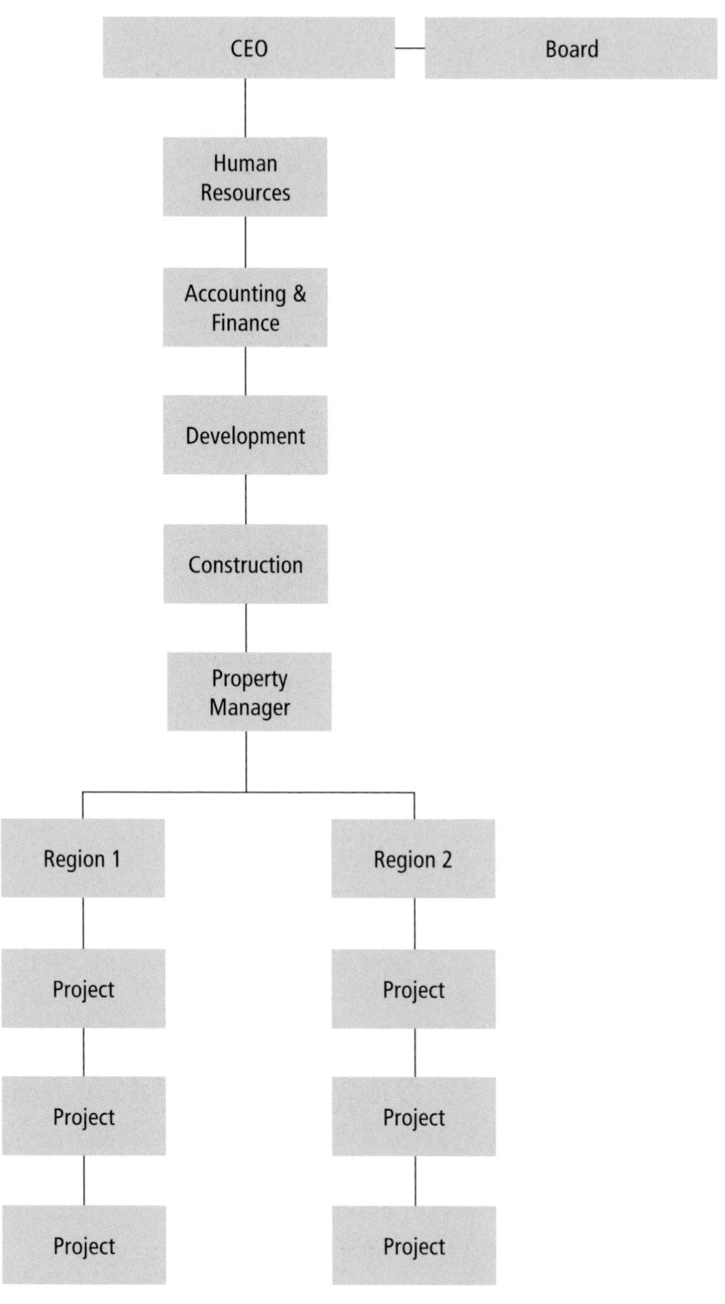

Figure 8-6: MATRIX ORGANIZATIONAL STRUCTURE

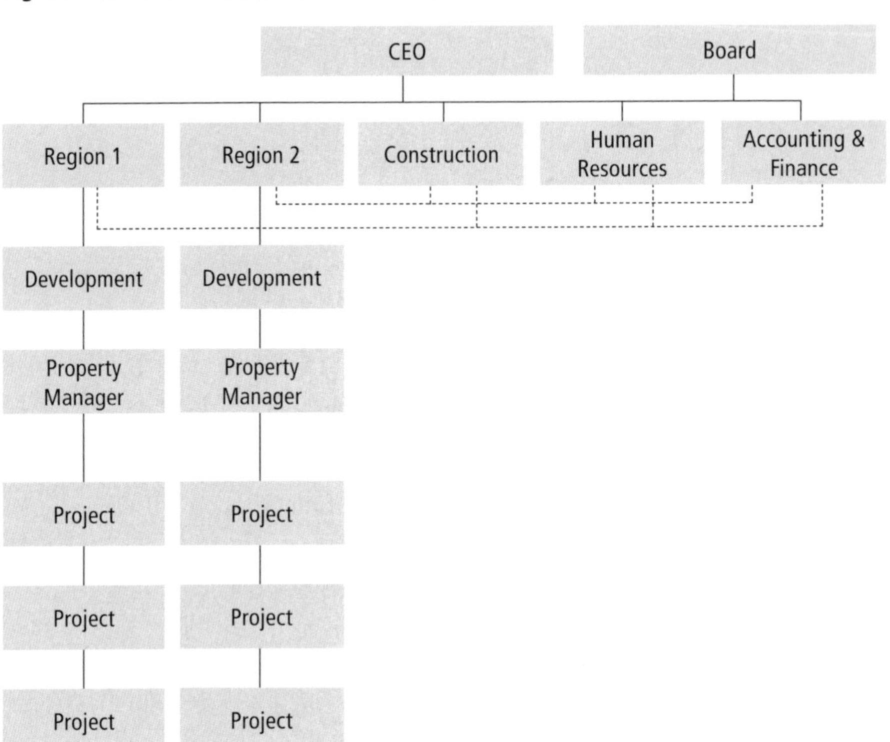

change occurs (or is expected), and a company then needs to put a new plan in place. Ideally, company leaders should engage in proactive succession planning before such an event takes place—particularly if it is one that can be anticipated, like the retirement of a key executive. All senior staff members—not just company leaders—must ask themselves, "Who will do my job next?"

Succession planning allows a company to make smooth transitions when executives and other key staff members retire or leave the firm. A company's leaders need to pay a great deal of attention to succession issues and should view succession planning as critically important to the firm's success. Companies that have consistent visions are able to make great progress in executing consistent strategies, while those that are constantly churning through managers have a much tougher time executing their strategies.

Every company seeking to create a stable, sustainable organization must have a succession plan in place for each of its senior staff members, with a line of sight to each person's replacement, whether that replacement involves promoting people from within the organization or hiring them from outside. If the company's head of construction were to be gone tomorrow, what would happen to the business? Is there a ready replacement inside the company who could take over in a reasonable period of time without a significant negative effect on the business? Could a person to fill this position be readily "hired in" from the outside? If not, the company needs to put in place strategies to ensure that an orderly transition will occur and begin working on these strategies diligently. Every manager, up and down the line, should be required to identify one or more candidates who are being trained to take over the manager's position—individuals who could, in five years or so, take over the manager's job and execute it successfully. Ideally, that manager should be on the candidate list of the person above, to take over his or her job as necessary. This is how an organization creates a healthy succession plan.

TYPICAL COMPONENTS OF EXECUTIVE COMPENSATION

Three-part total compensation package that consists of

1. Base Salary
2. Bonus—typically an annual performance bonus tied to a combination of individual and company performance measures, and in some cases a draw against long-term incentive compensation.
3. Long-Term Incentive Compensation—usually in the form of true equity or equity-like profit-sharing compensation tied to the performance of the company or division, individual projects, or portfolio.

Succession planning is more difficult to do in smaller companies, which have fewer layers of staff and thus do not have enough employees to have people continually in training. This is one of the reasons why relatively few small companies survive to see multiple generations of ownership and why owners of small companies who do have a legacy vision for their companies tend to adopt growth strategies relatively late in their careers, specifically to create "room" and opportunities for others to assume leadership positions within the company. The larger the company, the more critical it is to have succession planning in place, to identify the players, and to ensure that they are being trained and developed. Many real estate companies have not spent enough time and energy on this process and thus find themselves trying to catch up by doing not only succession planning but also leadership training, creating internal programs to home-grow leaders for management positions, even if those future leaders are not yet involved in management or are just beginning to be.

For the next decade or so, succession planning will be complicated by what many have dubbed "the lost generation" of real estate. The real estate depression that occurred across most of the United States from the late 1980s through the mid-1990s caused many to shun the industry, sending many business school graduates and other talented people who otherwise would have been rising through the ranks of the real estate industry to Wall Street, technology companies, and elsewhere—anywhere but real estate. For about a decade, from the late 1980s to the late 1990s, real estate as an industry category hired, trained, and developed very few managers. Therefore, when real estate companies started looking to hire talent as the industry recovered in the late 1990s and early years of the 21st century, the people they were looking for—those with five, six, seven years of experience—simply did not exist. Today, there are very few people in real estate with ten to 20 years of experience. Plenty of people have 30 or more years of experience and even more have fewer than ten years of experience, but the seasoned young manager with more than ten years of experience—the lifeline of a growing company—is a rare bird in today's market.

In the early years of the 21st century, the leaders at East West Partners realized that they had a group of leaders who had been together for about 20 years, but that there was a huge gap between that group—in terms of age, experience, and level of expertise—and the next younger group of managers. Because activity levels at East West Partners had been relatively low and the company had not experienced a lot of growth during the 1990s, the senior team was more than capable of handling all the company's work with the help of relatively junior people. During the 1990s, recognizing that that was the case, the rising stars at the company had left the firm to find work elsewhere. Thus, by the end of the 1990s, the group that had begun the decade in their forties were now in their fifties and older. The company had another group of managers who were in their twenties and early thirties, but nobody in their mid-thirties or forties with ten to 15 years of experience.

They immediately began to work on recreating their team, by inviting back managers who had left the company, creating opportunities for them—as well as new people—to grow, and designing training and development programs to engage them in management and leadership. Consequently, the company now has a significant leadership and succession training program in place. It has developed two layers of training and leadership development programs, one for the relatively junior thirty-something crowd and another for its relatively senior forty-something managers. Both programs help employees learn how to become better managers, get them involved with and engaged in the company's strategy and business planning processes, and expand the scale and breadth of their exposure to what the company does.

Succession planning also can involve making the transition from one form of ownership to another. Closely held private real estate organizations often are faced with making a transition from family-run or family-dominated leadership to professional nonfamily management and governance.

Compensation

For most real estate companies, a critical part of a strategic plan is the creation of a compensation system that enables them to attract and retain key talent while giving all members of the organization ample incentives to focus on achieving the company's strategic objectives. There are many different compensation systems, and no one formula works for all firms; each company must tailor its compensation plan to its strategy, structure, and personality.

Fixed versus Variable Compensation

The first issue deals with the extent to which the system is split between fixed compensation—base salary—and variable compensation—which typically includes an annual performance bonus and also may include longer-term incentive compensation, usually in the form of true equity or equity-like profit-sharing compensation that is tied to the performance of the company or division, individual projects, or a portfolio.

As a rule, the amount of total compensation is tied to the volume, throughput, and amount of responsibility that an individual has and his or her contribution to revenues and profitability. In general, the percentage of variable compensation increases with an employee's seniority and impact on profitability. Support and administrative staff, for example, may derive 95 percent of their anticipated total compensation from a base salary and 5 percent from variable compensation. For employees whose impact on profitability is considerably higher, the percentage of variable and long-term incentive compensation increases proportionately. For example, project managers who make a significant contribution to the firm's profitability may derive as much as 45 percent of their anticipated total compensation from a fixed base and 55 percent from a variable base, while a company's top executives may earn 70 percent of their annual income or more as variable compensation (figure 8-7). The amount of variable compensation typically increases exponentially as executives become more senior in the organization and take on more projects and more responsibility, and thus have more influence over profits.

EYA (formerly Eakin/Youngentob Associates), a medium-sized regional homebuilder that develops innovative urban communities in the Washington, D.C., metropolitan area, offers a good example of a compensation scheme on one end of the spectrum. The company's objective is to pay its key employees way above market rates, with the majority coming in the form of long-term incentive pay. This is done consciously to keep overhead down in periods of slow growth and align key employees' incentives with the owner's objectives of long-term wealth creation. EYA's total compensation therefore can be much higher than that of comparable companies, but that compensation is heavily "back ended" and is closely tied to the objectives of the organization and the success of its projects.

Today, compensation programs for senior real estate development executives typically fall into one of two camps: (a) a living wage with a big upside potential, as in the EYA example, in which the executive receives a competitive fixed annual compensation coupled with a much higher potential bonus or long-term incentive, or (b) a highly compensated annual salary with a decent upside potential, in which the executive's annual compensation is targeted at the 75th percentile or better, along with a more modest (but still generous) annual bonus and long-term incentive. Development executives increasingly are looking for more upside in value creation and are willing to take less in current income in exchange for a piece of the pie.

Long-term incentive compensation typically is a one-way street; that is, it has only an upside for those who participate, with no coinvestment commitment, capital calls, or personal guarantees. Many companies have a vesting formula for such compensation, which generally is graduated over a three- to five-year period or, in some cases, over a project's development and sell-out period. A

Figure 8-7: FIXED VERSUS VARIABLE COMPENSATION

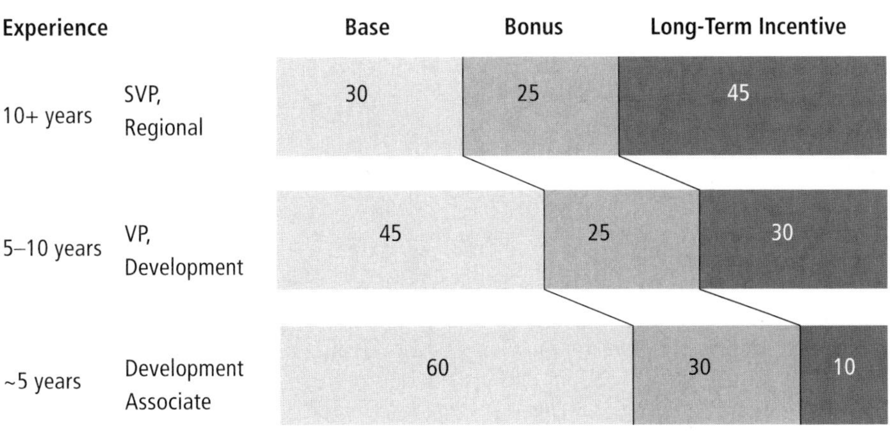

long-term incentive, even if it is not true equity, typically is portable, and executives who leave companies in good standing are entitled to their vested share. This practice means that employees are not "forced" to stick around, possibly being unproductive, while waiting for a project to pay off. Other companies, however, require executives to remain with the firm in order to collect their long-term incentive compensation. Some companies use a "netting" structure; if a manager has one project that makes money and another that loses money, he or she receives compensation based on the net profit of the two.

Quantitatively versus Qualitatively Formulated Compensation

The second issue is the extent to which the compensation system should be linked to quantitative and qualitative factors. Quantitative measures generally take the form of profit sharing or sales commissions for employees with profit and sales responsibility. Qualitative measures typically take the form of a "management by objective" system, by tracking subjective issues such as personnel training, morale, public relations, efficiency improvements, and customer satisfaction and rewarding them accordingly.

Most compensation systems tend to use some combination of quantitative and qualitative measures. Quantitative compensation measures often are oriented to the short term and account for annual sales and profits. They should be balanced by long-term qualitative measures. The split between quantitative and qualitative measures in the compensation system generally is weighted toward the quantitative—usually in the range of 60 percent or more—although the precise percentage is a matter of company preference.

In companies with long-term incentives that are heavily back ended, it can take a number of years for an individual's profit sharing to kick in. In the typical formula, when a company starts a new division, it lends the division working capital until the division starts breaking even and can cover its overhead. When the division starts selling deals and sees positive cash flow, it uses its first profits to pay back the working capital and invests additional profits in new deals. It typically takes seven to ten years for a division to build up sufficient profits to begin distributing them to its partners.

Publicly traded companies, including REITs, typically are not able to grant employees profit sharing or ownership stakes in individual real estate projects, but they are able to grant restricted shares of the company stock as a common element of their compensation programs. A number of public multifamily REITs have begun adopting compensation practices like those of private companies, tying the vesting of restricted stock options to project or division performance targets rather than just tenure; thus everyone is focused on pay for performance.

Individual versus Company Performance

Another variable is the extent to which compensation systems are designed to reward individual performance versus company performance. Most compensation systems are structured so that they do not pay any bonuses if the company does not earn money. When a company is profitable, the bulk of its compensation incentives typically are tied to individual performance, but there also generally is some tieback to the company's performance overall; this encourages teamwork and the sharing of best practices. Employees should have a stake in the projects for which they are responsible, but they also should have a vested interest in the performance of the company's entire portfolio. Roughly two-thirds or three-quarters of the bonus should reflect individual performance, with the balance based on the company's overall performance. This type of split tells employees that they are responsible for most of their bonus and that they must cooperate with their coworkers to earn the remainder. In other words, it provides the appropriate balance between personal incentive and corporate goodwill.

Many development companies structure this split by allowing or requiring those invited into the long-term incentive compensation program to have a stake in every deal or project in the division or, in some cases, the company. They do so to promote collaboration and cooperation throughout the company and to avoid encouraging executives to focus only on the deals or projects in which they may have a personal stake, to the detriment of the company's other projects and deals.

Overall, the structure of a compensation program is less important than tying compensation—whatever form it takes—to performance. The fundamental truth is that people respond to incentives. What the company cares about is the long-term profitability and success of its projects. Incentive compensation should be tied in part—ideally, in large part—to the long-term performance of the company's projects. This can be accomplished through real ownership of a company's assets (which may not be desirable, or even possible) or through "phantom" ownership, in which benchmarks are set for a project's expected profitability and incentive compensation is tied to reaching or exceeding those benchmarks. Ideally, compensation payments also will be tied to when those benchmarks are achieved, so that individuals are paid at the same time the company is paid. In the meantime, it is important to ensure that people earn a living wage and can sustain their lifestyle between bonuses or long-term incentive payments. Balancing the two forms of compensation is an art, not a science.

Growth and Organizational Expansion

During the upturn phase of the real estate cycle, a company's managers must determine how to structure and staff a growing organization. For example, when expanding into new markets, should the company move senior managers from the locations where they are working to new markets—as "pioneers"—or should it hire new managers who already know the new market—local "sharpshooters"—and teach them company systems and culture? Local sharpshooters already know the geography, have the contacts, and do not have to pay the proverbial "dumb tax" of learning the market; they can hit the ground running. However, they need systems, capital, and organizational support. Pioneers—experienced, cherished employees who already are inculcated with the corporate culture—will need to learn the new market, but they bring with them some organizational capabilities on which they can build the business in that market. Again, these are two bookends; most firms' techniques fall somewhere between them.

Another way to enter a new market is to buy a company or operation that is already in the market, which may even have an ongoing flow of deals. This method also allows the company to hit the ground running. Homebuilders have done this all over the United States; as they have grown, their typical preference has been not to send a manager to a new market to start a new division but rather to buy a smaller homebuilder in that market and integrate it into their organization.

There are pros and cons to all three alternatives. The benefits of buying an existing company are that it allows the company to ramp up immediately, with existing inventory, work flow, and deal flow. The gearing-up time is minimal; a company gets an almost instant presence in the new market. If the buyer has chosen wisely, the purchased company will continue to operate well and its performance will improve with the addition of whatever the purchaser brings to the deal, which may include capital, industry knowledge, exposure, innovation, or operating systems. An acquired company may have some great features that can be exported to the rest of the acquiring organization.

The downsides include the fact that the leader of the acquired company may not adapt well to new ownership. That individual often ends up leaving and must be replaced. Acquired firms do not necessarily have the depth of management to enable someone within the organization to take over. As a result, there is often a transition within a year or two or three that involves a significant shakeup of existing managers and an infusion of people from other divisions or locations to keep the operation going. An acquired company typically has its own culture, which may not be consistent with that of the acquiring organization; it may be difficult to integrate the two. Operational integration also may be difficult to accomplish; the firms' systems, procedures, approaches, and methodologies may not mesh well and could require time-consuming and potentially expensive changes. Some who have experienced merger and acquisition integration firsthand describe the process as being akin to trying to change the tires on a car while driving 60 miles per hour down the highway.

The benefit of sending pioneers into a new market is that they already know the company very well. The downside is that it will take them time to learn that market. There is a very good chance that their early transactions will not be preferred transactions; they may overpay for land, not understand local building codes, design projects that require multiple change orders during the construction process, not know the local vendors and contractors and thus pay extra for a lower-quality product than perhaps a local player would have gotten during the development and construction process. The entitlement and approval process can be expected to go more slowly. Costs will go up and speed will go down, compared with an individual's performance in his or her home market. But there is no question that understanding the organization, its culture, and its products, is a plus.

The advantages of hiring local sharpshooters are the exact opposite. Local experts should have local knowledge. They should be able to locate and do deals faster; they should know the local building communities and be able to get projects designed, approved, built, marketed, and managed successfully. The downside to hiring local sharpshooters, as with an acquisition, are cultural and systems integration. It takes time to build an organization around an individual; doing so may drain resources from the home office; and a company runs the risk of poor communication. Mistakes may be made as a result of the new manager's lack of understanding of how the company operates. Even if a company decides that hiring a local sharpshooter is the way to go, it may have a hard time finding the right person. Individuals who are not tied up in back-ended, long-term incentive compensation programs may be few and far between, and breaking those people loose from their commitments is not easy—or inexpensive. Thus an additional benefit of a long-term compensation plan, as discussed in the preceding section, is that it makes it less likely that key employees will be lured away by other offers.

Real estate remains a largely local business. Because it can be difficult to teach an old dog new tricks, acquiring an operation or hiring someone who already understands a new market may be more effective than moving someone to the new market, particularly if the company adopts a project orientation. Yet a company that is more process oriented, that has a unique culture and history and possibly systems and processes unlike those of other companies, may have a difficult time finding a local sharpshooter who can fit in. This may or may not be important; perhaps the company worries less about inculcating new managers with its culture and instead adapts to incorporate the new manager's culture as the organization expands. These are all issues that all companies should address. An organization needs to determine what the best approach is for its unique situation as it looks to expand into new markets or new segments.

South Group, a venture of two successful Portland-based residential developers —Williams & Dame Development and Gerding-Edlen Development—provides an example of the process. The two firms understood multifamily housing and Portland and took their show on the road to downtown Los Angeles. They formed the venture to lessen the risk of entering a new market. The challenge was to enter the market when few local developers displayed much vision. Based on knowledge of the downtown Portland market, the venture made the decision to enter the downtown Los Angeles market with a three-phased development that in the middle of the first decade of the 21st century was the single largest program of new condo construction in the market. The product has been well received, and the success has demonstrated market acceptance of urban living in downtown Los Angeles. The two firms have found additional market opportunities in Los Angeles outside the downtown area. They no longer need to work together, each having become comfortable with its capabilities and new alliances.

The Final Word

When exploring which organizational strategies are most appropriate, a company should be careful to not let its current organizational structure and staff resources dictate the approach to and results of the strategic planning process. Senior staff members should take a step back and attempt to start from scratch (at least intellectually), rather than with the company's existing structure. Organizational charts should be drawn up with positions and functions but without individual's names, at least initially, to ensure that decisions are not unduly influenced by whom the company has on staff at a given moment.

Senior staff should first design the ideal organizational chart that will enable the company to execute its mission and vision and to be effective in its markets, its product or service segments, and its chosen industry roles. Then, this ideal should be compared with the company's existing structure, to identify gaps and to chart a path to the optimal organizational structure. Wholesale and rapid organizational change can be disruptive and counterproductive to a company's success, and it may be advisable to take several interim steps as a company makes a transition from its current state to the optimal one.

HAPTER 9

Capital Strategies

Capital strategies define how a company will access and deploy capital to achieve its goals and objectives and fund its chosen industry roles. Real estate financing typically is focused on capital risk roles, given the capital-intense nature of these activities compared with operating risk roles. Specifically, it is concentrated on the rapid value creation made possible by assuming the riskiest industry roles—such as land speculation, land development, building development, and acquisition of existing assets—and on the modest value enhancement that occurs during the holding of stabilized assets (figure 9-1). Most of the value typically is created by playing the riskiest industry roles, before an asset is stabilized.

Real estate companies that want to create value rapidly through capital risk roles, especially the highest-risk ones, are well advised to consider using operating risk businesses as their foundations, in order to generate a stable, diversified income stream that can allow the company to weather interruptions in the real estate or capital market cycles. It has been proven time and time again that tremendous benefits accrue to a diversified company that generates profits and cash flow from operating risk businesses, as well as creating value through capital risk activities (figure 9-2).

Figure 9-1: INCOME-PRODUCING ASSETS VALUE CHAIN

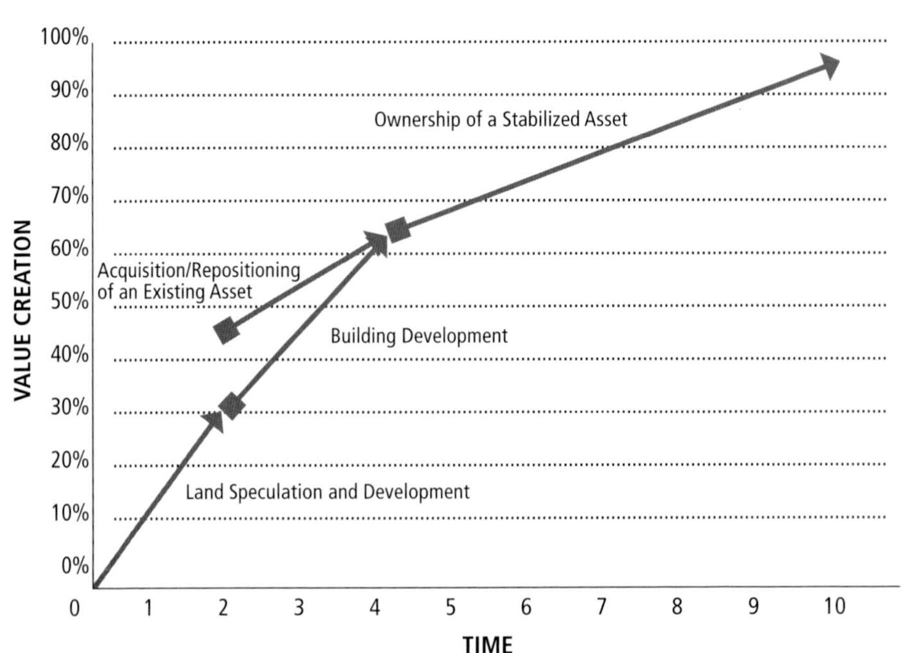

REITs do a very good job—by necessity—of creating a stable operating environment. But any type of company, public or private, can follow this healthy model of an asset base that produces ongoing cash flow that is free and clear of the servicing debt and thus available to reinvest in properties or to fund projects in the pipeline or acquisitions. This is a solid, tried and true way to do business. Some of the wealthiest families in the real estate world—the Pritzkers, the Shorensteins, the Ratners, the Galbreaths, the Carrs—started out with this model. The patriarchs of these families had the foresight to be net buyers and not sellers; they did not have a trading mentality. Over the years, they built portfolios of income-producing assets with hundreds of thousands of apartments and millions of square feet of office, retail, and industrial space. Those portfolios still generate significant cash flows, which allowed them—and now their offspring—to reinvest in acquisitions and development and continue to grow and flourish.

gure 9-2: LAND DEVELOPMENT VALUE CHAIN CREATION

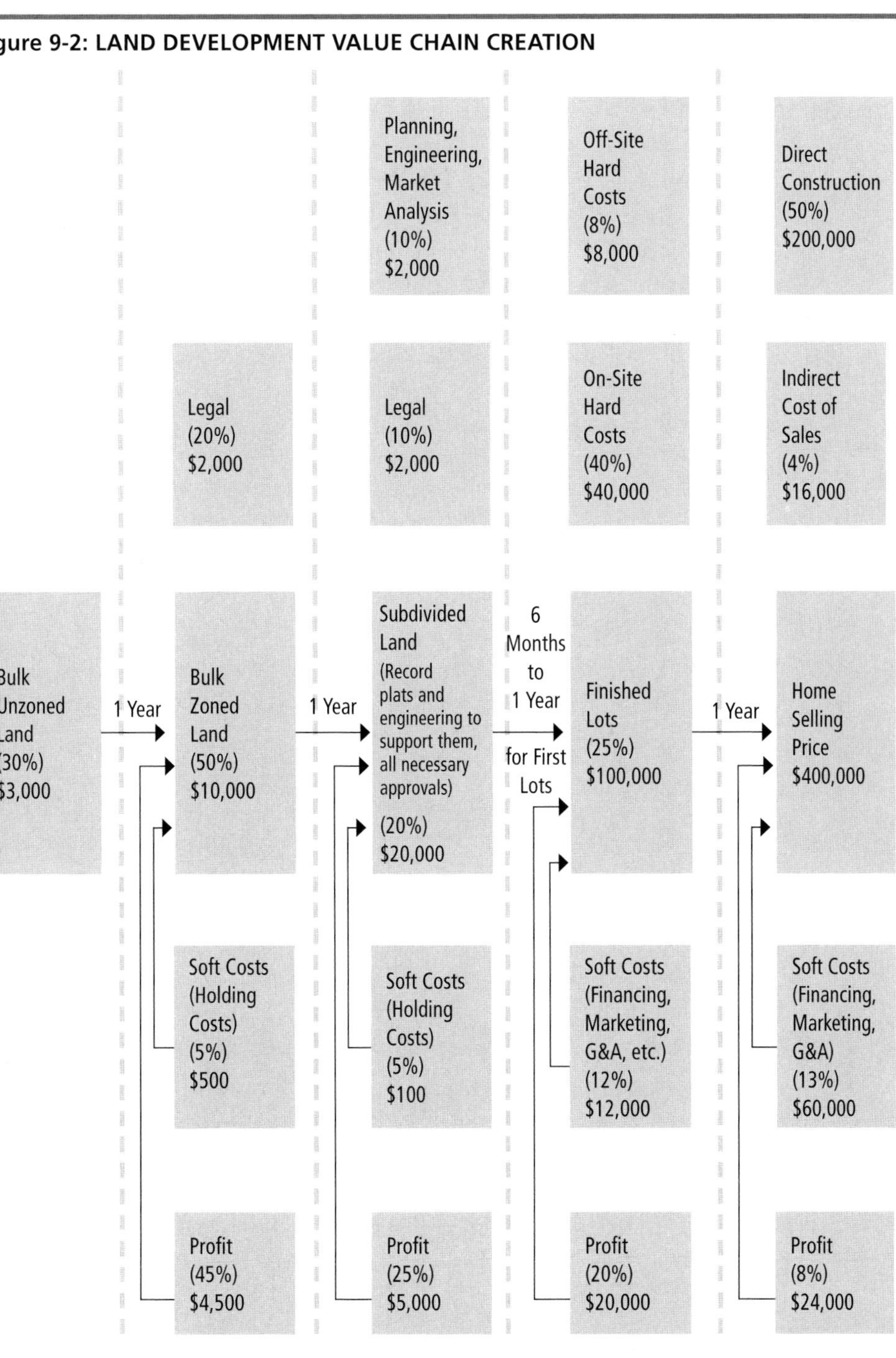

CHAPTER 9

An Iterative Process

Capital strategies define how a company accesses, manufactures, and deploys capital to reach its goals and achieve its strategic objectives. The discussion here of capital strategies is purposefully positioned at the end of the list of strategy pillars that a real estate company should build on. The availability of capital—or, more likely, the perception of capital constraints—should not drive the strategic planning process. A company's strategy should instead be informed by an iterative process that carefully examines the company's capital needs and potential capital sources and helps prioritize its capital formation and allocation activities.

First, a company should determine what it is going to do, what roles it should play, and where it is going to pursue opportunities—all informed by the opportunities and constraints in the marketplace. Then it should figure out how to finance those activities. Rather than saying, "Here is how much money we have to play with—now what should we do with it?" the underlying assumption should be that the resources necessary to execute a good strategy—including human capital and financial capital—can be obtained. Having said this, some capital constraints typically do come into play, and the formation of capital strategies should be an iterative process that dovetails with and informs other aspects of a company strategy. It is perfectly legitimate to modify and amend decisions regarding industry role, geographic deployment, and other strategies after careful consideration of what capital and cost of capital can reasonably be applied. But it is important to ensure that artificial constraints do not color what is open for consideration.

For some "commodity" real estate products or in highly competitive asset acquisition and long-term hold situations, obtaining capital at the lowest cost possible is a critical aspect of a company's capital formation strategy. For most real estate companies, however, capital formation strategies do not need to focus exclusively on finding the cheapest capital. Instead they should focus on ensuring consistent access to a cost-effective and predictable source, or sources, of capital that enable the company to conduct its business in all phases of the real estate cycle.

The goal should be to identify the best capital source and the optimal capital structure for the company. The best capital source is not necessarily the cheapest.

What makes a capital source best for a particular company? Three characteristics: It should be competitively priced and cost-effective; it should be dependable and consistent; and it should assert the least amount of unwanted or unneeded control over the company possible. Real estate company leaders want capital to be available whenever they need it, not only when the capital source wants to make it available. Real estate executives also want to maintain as much control of their businesses as possible; they do not want their capital sources dictating their business. They want capital sources that allow them to take reasonable risks without jeopardizing the rest of their activities. Some operators want to contain risk through their capital structure and may not want a problem in a specific market, project, or other situation to necessarily affect the rest of their operations or portfolio.

A number of companies purposefully use project-level financing—recognizing that it is not necessarily the least expensive capital available—to mitigate the risk that troubles at one project could take down a number of other projects or the entire company. A project-level financing strategy thus is also a risk containment strategy. If troubles emerge on any one project, only that project is in jeopardy, not the whole organization. The ultimate entity-level financing vehicle is the public REIT. The classic example of a company getting into trouble is the situation in which all the company's assets are individually financed but cross-collateralized. When trouble begins to surface with some of the assets, these troubles trigger a domino effect of compliance issues not only for the underperforming assets but also for the company's other assets, causing all the dominoes to fall. Many private companies have determined that it is best to finance each asset on an individual basis without any cross-collateralization. That can prove difficult to accomplish, because of the question of security. It is a balancing act. It is easier to accomplish in a very low-leverage environment but hard to accomplish in a high-leverage environment.

How do companies evolve from recourse, cross-collateralization financing to nonrecourse, project-level financing? The way to get off recourse is either to have a relatively low level of leverage, so as to provide the lender sufficient security at the property level even in the case of a diminution of the valuation, or to enhance the borrower's credit. The borrower's credit and performance record also play an important role in reducing the personal obligation and eliminating cross-collateralization requirements. The stronger the borrower is, in terms of having a long history of successful, profitable development and no defaults, the easier it is for that borrower to get requirements for personal guarantees and cross-collateralization waived and to obtain credit enhancement, if necessary.

Today's sophisticated, highly specialized credit markets draw capital market players who will accept the liability for just about anything, for a price. Credit enhancement may help increase borrowing capacity at a relatively modest cost, particularly when compared with the cost of outside equity. To enhance its credit, the borrower typically sets aside a pool of funds that serve as the first source of repayment in case of trouble. After that pool is exhausted, the credit enhancer steps in to accept the liabilities. The price of credit enhancement is set as a percentage of the contingent obligation. Although it is not free, credit enhancement is an attractive way to reduce risk and gain peace of mind for those who cannot otherwise avoid providing personal guarantees and cross-collateralization provisions.

The Bozzuto Group seriously reevaluated its capital acquisition strategies as part of a major strategic planning process. In the mid-1990s, the firm, which was generally risk averse and operated through joint ventures, determined that it was paying too much for money and taking on too much risk. By expanding and diversifying the nature and number of its institutional partners, Bozzuto was able to reduce its risk and obtain financing on better terms. By 2007, the organization had completed deals with new capital providers such as the New York State Teachers' Retirement System, Fannie Mae, and Prudential Equity Group.

Potential Capital Sources

The broad range of capital sources available to real estate companies includes banks, insurance companies, pension funds, private equity funds, REITs, foundations, and even individuals. In order to develop a capital formation strategy, real estate companies must understand that different types of investors have different needs. On the debt side, banks, by regulation, must make loans for a short period of time. They are, therefore, one of the primary sources of shorter-term loans, primarily construction and mini-perm loans. Some institutions, such as insurance companies, will make permanent loans to keep in their own portfolios or to sell to the secondary loan market. On the equity side, REITs, foundations, university endowments, insurance companies, and pension funds typically have well-defined, predictable short-, medium-, and long-term cash flow needs. Individual and family investors often look ahead many generations for sustainable returns. Most investors, however, use the typical methodology—biased toward the short term, based on discounted cash flow—when evaluating real estate investments because this is how they were taught to evaluate alternative investments in business school.

Understanding the Capital Source's Motivation; Finding the Right Sources

In the purest economic sense, gaining access to capital involves optimizing the risk-adjusted return for the benefit of the source of the capital. Other elements of a capital source's strategy and goals, however, can offer compelling arguments for why that source might consider its risk-adjusted return to be higher than the actual rate of return it receives from an investment in a particular real estate company or project.

Real estate companies should recognize that capital sources are motivated by a wide range of goals and issues. Although all capital sources aim to maximize the return on their investment, some also may have other goals. They may be interested in investing in a particular product type or a specific geographic area, or they may want to become involved in urban revitalization, green development, transit-oriented development, or workforce housing. They may derive intangible benefits from investing in high-profile projects or companies and may be willing to accept lower returns if they believe that their risk is lower when investing in a certain project or with a certain sponsor. In short, while the capital markets are quick to quote a price and terms, deals rarely get executed at the quoted price and with the quoted terms. Because capital sources take into account the factors noted above, they actually vary their prices and terms from deal to deal.

Real estate companies that have a specific focus should seek out like-minded capital sources, since a capital source aiming to penetrate a specific product segment or market area—or with particular social goals—might be prepared to accept a lower return on its investment or to provide terms that are more attractive to the real estate company, particularly if the firm has a strong reputation, market presence, or brand. Themed investment funds—those set up to invest in a particular field, such as land transactions, environmentally sensitive projects, environmental remediation efforts, or urban revitalization—are one place to find investors who understand those types of projects, who are willing to take the risks involved in underwriting them, and who as a result may have different investment and return criteria than traditional lenders. This does not necessarily mean that the money provided by these funds will be less expensive or less restrictive, although it could be. But using a specialized lender or investor should take time and cost out of the underwriting process. These investors understand the field and should be able to evaluate a company or a project more quickly, underwrite the assets, and determine whether they are comfortable making the investment.

One such example is Revival Funds, a proposed $200 million private real estate equity fund with an exclusive focus on urban green projects. Because this is considered a relatively new market niche—and hence priced accordingly—Revival Funds will offer equity that initially will be priced lower than the competition, in anticipation that in the medium to long run, these investments will produce returns that are significantly above average.

Another example is Arcadia Land Company, which engages only in joint ventures with landowners who share the company's new urbanist, sustainable approach to residential development. Arcadia has, for example, entered a joint venture with a well-to-do, old-line Philadelphia family on land the family has owned for generations. The family contributed this land to the Arcadia projects because both entities share common values about developing walkable projects that also preserve the maximum practical amount of land as open space.

One Source or Several?

Is a real estate company better off relying on a single capital source, or should it have multiple capital sources? Put simply, would you rather dance with an 800-pound gorilla or a bunch of monkeys? Each approach has plusses and minuses. Working with one capital source can be much more efficient than managing relationships with several. And it can be much more difficult for real estate executives to form relationships with multiple capital sources, when those sources know the executives are talking to other sources as well. On the flip side, relying on a single capital source could be disastrous if that source suddenly decides it no longer wants to invest in a company or its projects, and the company has no other source lined up. When the gorilla decides to stop dancing, you will not be able to make it start again.

One homebuilding company chose to get its funding solely through one of the company partners, a pension advisory firm that funded its investment through a particular pension fund. The company developed a growth strategy and an implementation plan. While that plan was being implemented, the pension advisory firm decided to close out the fund. That decision compelled the rest of the company's partners—who still believed in the plan and wanted to give it a chance to succeed—to liquidate the company at values well below what they probably could have realized if they had seen the business plan through to its conclusion and waited until then to sell the company. Even though the majority of the partners wanted to keep dancing, when the capital source decided to sit down, they all had to go home.

Here again, East West Partners is a good example of a real estate company that has relied primarily on a single capital source. For more than ten years, East West Partners had an excellent relationship with a single primary capital source, Crescent Real Estate Equities Company, one of the nation's largest REITs. Crescent invested more than $250 million in East West Partners projects. In addition to being a dependable, deep-pocketed source of well-priced capital that had a tremendous amount of trust and confidence in the company's management ability, Crescent also was extremely helpful in bringing projects and deals that East West Partners might not have discovered on its own. Over the years, the company's leaders discussed whether relying on a single capital source was a safe strategy or whether they should be looking for alternative sources, but ultimately they always decided that as long as the relationship with Crescent remained beneficial to both parties, they would stick with it. One day, Crescent decided to pull out. Although East West Partners was able to identify alternative capital sources relatively quickly and make an orderly shift to those sources, the situation could have resulted in a huge meltdown. Luckily for the company, Crescent's decision occurred at a time when the market was relatively liquid and plenty of capital was available. Imagine if Crescent had decided to pull out when the real estate capital markets dried up, as they were in the early 1990s.

The lesson to be learned here is to choose partners carefully. This applies to financial partners as much as—if not more than—other partners. Chief financial officers and other executives must know and understand their capital sources, what motivates those sources to invest in a company or project, and what might cause those sources to stop investing. They need to understand what impact a change in their capital sources' strategies or circumstances could have on their business and work those potential impacts into their decision-making processes. In other words, you need to know what you are going to do if your partner stops dancing before you are ready to leave the floor.

Operating Risk Business Finance

All operating risk and process-oriented businesses, in real estate and in many other industries, have similar financial structures. The funds that are permanently invested in the business—whether it is property management, construction management, or some other operating risk business—represent the working capital required to run the company on a day-to-day basis. The one exception is general contracting. In addition to the permanent investment in the business of working capital, general contracting typically requires bonding, which may require tying up capital to secure a standby letter of credit.

Working capital is the bridge funding that covers the time gap between the immediate obligations of payroll, rent, and other accounts payable and the receipt of the company's fees. This time gap generally is between 55 and 90 "day sales," a figure that is calculated as the firm's annual revenue divided by 365 days, or approximately 15 percent to 25 percent of annual billings. A company can reduce its working capital needs, sometimes substantially, by putting in place an efficient and timely collections process and by asking for partial prepayment of services (retainers). Such actions can reduce the amount of working capital to 12 percent to 18 percent of annual billings. In other words, the company that operates efficiently and is able to secure partial prepayments can permanently invest between $0.12 and $0.18 of each dollar of working capital in the company.

The primary reason that a fast-growing operating risk business fails is a shortage of working capital. A rapidly expanding operating risk business often outstrips its ability to generate sufficient working capital internally. If a company does not understand the importance of working capital, it soon will face the day when it cannot make its payroll.

For example, if an asset management business has annual revenues of $100 million, it needs approximately $20 million (20 percent of revenues) in permanently invested working capital. If the company has a 5 percent pretax margin (or $5 million), it could grow by an additional $15 million[1] in revenues during the next year by using internally generated funds, assuming the owners did not take money out of the business. If the asset management business grew by more than $15 million in revenues, it would have to raise outside capital to meet its payroll and other daily expenditures or else risk financial difficulties.

A developer who successfully entered the property management business in the Southwest during the late 1980s learned about the importance of working capital, though the lesson almost put the company into bankruptcy. After establishing a base of 5 million square feet under management, partly the company's own product and partly a third-party product under management, the developer landed a large government contract to manage an additional 4 million square feet of space. Unaware of how slowly the government pays, the developer faced a serious cash flow squeeze within weeks of assuming management responsibility. Only a hastily arranged line of credit from the bank (ironically, the government contract collateralized the line) saved the firm from possible bankruptcy.

Because it eliminates the need for outside partners or debt, internally generated working capital is the best way to expand an operating risk business.

The Final Word

Although it is useful to divide the financing of real estate companies into capital risk and operating risk components, bringing these two components back together can help a company engage safely in capital risk roles. Real estate companies do not need to take on both capital risk and operating risk roles—and, indeed, many have succeeded by taking on only capital risk roles—yet taking on both roles still represents a well-balanced strategy. Doing so may become increasingly important for companies that will face changes in the real estate markets and possible future dislocations in the capital markets.

Endnote

[1] $5 million less $2 million for taxes at 40 percent equals $3 million, divided by 20 percent equals $15 million.

CHAPTER 10

Cycle Strategies

Cycle strategies, sometimes referred to as downsizing or rationalization strategies, are typically the opposite of growth strategies. These strategies usually are pursued during the mature phase of the real estate cycle and take on added importance during the downturn phase.

Some companies conduct business in anticipation of cycles. They understand that real estate is a cyclical business. While they will be the first to admit that they do not know when the cycles will happen, they finance and staff their businesses knowing that they will in fact happen. From a staffing perspective, this means that they outsource—rather than internalize—all the services they reasonably can.

Often, the best time to be in the vertical building business is during the downturn. This is when land sellers are eager to unload excess inventory, and it is typically when developers and builders who are able to finance their activities can secure the cheapest costs, the best sites, and so forth.

Builders and investors must recognize that development projects usually take three years or longer to cycle from concept to delivery. Consequently, there is a very good chance that any given project will be delivered into a downturn. In many of today's supply-constrained markets, developers cannot wait to start a project when they see that the market is recovering; then it is too late. Rather, they need to have been working on the deal for two or three years before they can secure the necessary entitlement and financing to start construction. Trammell Crow Residential has this exact philosophy about operating in a highly cyclical business. According to Ron Terwilliger, "what we have to do is build a project in a good location at today's costs, and finance it so that if the market for rental apartments is bad when we deliver it, we can hold it until the market recovers. The only thing that would shut us down would be a lack of acceptable financing."

Cycle strategies determine how a company will anticipate, monitor, plan for, and act in a downturn (and the inevitable recovery) or under other adverse conditions. They also govern what the company will do when events, external or internal, do not go according to plan and an adverse situation emerges. They question the company's every geographic market, product or service, market segment, and industry role. Although cycle strategies rarely are a favorite topic, they are critical to the survival of a company during a real estate recession or depression. A company that waits until the market has shifted into a downturn phase to begin to think about cycle strategies probably has waited too long and could be in for a rough ride. Conversely, a company with a clever cycle strategy can benefit greatly from the misfortune of others and from the dislocations and economic inefficiencies that inevitably accompany periods of uncertainty and instability in the market.

DEFENSIVE CYCLE STRATEGIES

- Insulate from need to lose assets
- Weather downturns

Examples:

- Tightening geographic focus
- Tightening underwriting criteria
- Delay, drop deals (more severe)
- Redeploy financial or human capital
- Cut overhead
- Mergers and acquisitions

Defensive Strategies

Defensive cycle strategies insulate a company from the need to lose key assets and enable it to weather a downturn (see box at left). Examples of defensive strategies include narrowing a company's geographic focus, tightening its underwriting criteria, redeploying financial or human capital, cutting overhead, and limiting mergers and acquisitions. In a more severe downturn, they also may include shedding industry roles and delaying or even walking away from deals.

Another set of defensive cycle strategies includes diversifying and maintaining a conservative financial posture and a healthy balance sheet, which can insulate a company and help it weather a downturn. For example, Collier Enterprises, a private rental apartment developer, owner, and operator primarily of student housing communities in Gainesville, Florida, has adopted a series of defensive cycle strategies. They include maintaining a minimum liquidity of $5 million to $10 million, diversifying beyond its core Gainesville market, adding more conventional (not student) apartments to its portfolio, keeping no more than 10 percent of its portfolio in development properties, and maintaining a conservative debt posture, by holding long-term, ten-year fixed-rate, nonrecourse debt with staggered maturities that are not cross-collateralized.

Offensive Strategies

Offensive cycle strategies help position a company to take advantage of the market opportunities that inevitably present themselves during a downturn (see box at right). Maintaining a strong balance sheet can be an effective defensive strategy to help a company survive difficult or lean times, but it also can create a war chest that can be used offensively to take advantage of opportunities that arise. Other examples of offensive cycle strategies include capital formation and deal-sourcing strategies to take advantage of attractive sell-off opportunities.

OFFENSIVE CYCLE STRATEGIES

- Position company to take advantage of market opportunities

Examples:
- Maintain strong balance sheet
- Capital formation and deal sourcing strategies to take advantage of attractive sell-off opportunities

The conversion of many multifamily companies into REITs in the early 1990s was an effective use of capital formation as both a defensive and an offensive cycle strategy. Faced with declining market fundamentals and a lack of liquidity available to the private sector, many private rental apartment companies went public as REITs, as a means to recapitalize their portfolios (without which step many might have gone under). They then used their access to public market equity to consolidate and take advantage of other operators that were under stress.

Market Monitoring

Being able to predict and anticipate downturns or other adverse conditions with clarity would be ideal, but many—both inside and outside the industry—do not believe it is possible to have this type of 20/20 forward vision. That does not mean, however, that companies should not be in touch with the pulse of the economy and the real estate market. Every company should put in place processes (formal or informal) to monitor the marketplace and their business and, most important, should have strategies in place and the discipline to act differently in the face of changing conditions. Having some type of monitoring process in place and a set of strategy actions at the ready is what distinguishes great companies from not-so-great (or out-of-business) companies.

As one senior real estate professional said in August 2007, "You cannot predict downturns; you can observe them, but you never see them coming. They come from things you couldn't predict or imagine. We could be in a recession right now because of problems in the subprime mortgage sector. Who knows? Every downturn is different. They're spaced differently. I believe they're unanticipatable —which doesn't mean you don't monitor, because you'll see early warning signs. But saying definitively that you know the next downturn's going to be 2010 and let's plan accordingly, I think that's naïve."

Early Warning System

Putting in place processes to monitor economic and real estate market conditions is essential; not doing so can result in a lack of focus or in inertia, both of which may prevent a company from recognizing changing market conditions. The first and most important step is to know when the market has shifted into the next phase of the cycle. It is easy to acknowledge the recession six to 12 months after it has begun, but by then it may be too late. Companies that wait until it is clear that their current growth strategies are no longer applicable before preparing and deploying cycle strategies probably have waited too long.

Some companies make a significant commitment in both time and money to developing and deploying a proactive, state-of-the-art monitoring and early warning system designed to systemically measure and track economic and market data, thereby assisting their management teams in making their timing calls. Other companies lack the resources to invest heavily in market monitoring systems and, instead, rely on readily available secondary sources of economic and market data. Many more simply rely on anecdotal information and their intuition. Whatever the level and sophistication of the input, it is critical that a company's leadership regularly convene a forum—at least quarterly, or more frequently if the outlook is uncertain or volatile—to determine where the company is in the economic and real estate cycle and what, if anything, the company should do differently in the execution of its strategy. As noted at the beginning of this chapter, a conscious consensus among the leaders of the company has tremendous value.

Companies that invest in a market monitoring system tend to select a set of leading and coincident indicators that are most relevant to the company's business and to the geographic markets in which it operates. Typically, the set includes national economic indicators, metropolitan area economic indicators, capital market indicators, national real estate market indicators, metropolitan area real estate market indicators, and individual company performance factors (figure 10-1). These data then are fed into an analytical system that tests them against a set of measures; data that fail to meet the test trigger consideration of a particular course of action.

Very often, a company's internal information about its operations, customers, or portfolio can provide the best indicators of change in the marketplace. It is often much more timely and relevant than general economic indicators, such as the Consumer Confidence Index, building permits, and job growth, which tend to lag in reporting. For example, a homebuilder's internal weekly traffic report is current information from which any changes in the direction of activity can be immediately determined, whereas it may take weeks or even months to learn that marketwide sales or permits are down.

Trigger Events

Companies should establish trigger events—when the data fail to meet the test—for each measure or possibly for combinations of measures, to provide the guidance for taking specific actions as the probability of a downturn increases, rather than relying on a single metric to predict a recession. Indicators from several categories should be selected for their historic reliability, relevance to the company, availability on a timely basis, and rationality. Collier Enterprises, for example, tracks a set of indicators that includes declining leasing trends (across

Figure 10-1: REAL ESTATE CYCLE INDICATORS

National Economic Indicators
- Consumer expectations
- Change in gross domestic product
- Real income growth
- Factory output
- Industrial inventories
- Corporate profits
- Employment growth
- Trends relating to key national industries
- Shape of yield curve
- Stock market valuation
- Energy costs
- Trade deficit
- Hours worked by average worker

Capital Indicators
- Capitalization rates
- Personal debt levels
- Cost of capital (including interest rates)
- Mortgage default rates

Metropolitan Area Real Estate Market Indicators
- Residential building permits
- Home sales and price trends
- Land values and transaction volumes
- Property values and transaction volume trends
- Capitalization rates
- Construction spending
- Lot inventory
- Vacancy rates
- Pipeline versus projected demand
- Occupancy rates (office, retail, apartment, hotel)
- Rental rate and price trends
- Relationship of home price to income

Metropolitan Area Economic Indicators
- Consumer expectations or confidence
- Stock price changes for group of leading companies with significant presence in the metropolitan area
- Retail sales of durable goods
- Trends relating to key metropolitan area industries
- Employment, particularly in key sectors (e.g., textiles)
- Unemployment rates
- Construction employment as a percentage of total employment
- Migration data
- Visitor data
- Business expansions and relocations
- Initial claims for unemployment insurance

National Real Estate Market Indicators
- Building permit data
- Home sales
- Occupancy rates (office, retail, apartment, hotel)
- Rental rate and price trends

Company Performance Factors
(Indicators specific to a company's operations)
- Absorption and leasing activity
- Occupancy
- Rent trends and sale prices
- Traffic counts
- Cancellations
- Transactions

its entire portfolio) compared with the preceding year, concessions in the market, rising capitalization rates, broker information, and insurance and tax trends. When a combination of these factors reaches a specific threshold, the company interprets that as the first trigger event, which in turn stimulates the management team to consider implementing its first level of strategic response.

Trigger events and corresponding cycle strategy actions should be designed in stages, to avoid overreacting to minor or temporary changes in the indicators. At the same time, the stages should be sensitive enough that the first event—and the actions a company takes in response, which may include simply increasing its awareness or vigilance and continuing to monitor the indicators for further deterioration—is not delayed to the point at which the market, and the company, might already be in trouble.

Figure 10-2: CYCLE STRATEGY STAGES

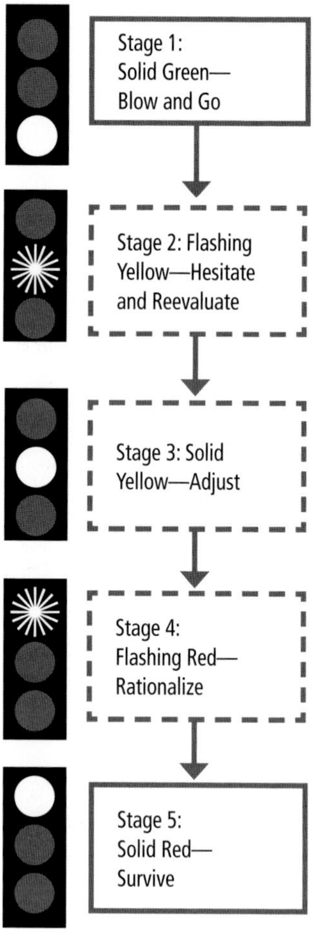

Cycle Strategy Stages

Each company faces a unique set of circumstances, in terms of product types, industry roles, geographic deployment, and so forth. Therefore no one cycle strategy and market monitoring system works for every company or situation. The market monitoring and trigger event processes identified in figure 10-2 by traffic light colors illustrate the types of systems developed by companies with which we are familiar.

Solid Green: Blow and Go

During the upturn and early mature phases of the real estate cycle, when all a company's indicators are positive, the cycle strategy status is "solid green light." The company is pursuing growth strategies, not cycle strategies. As it does so, however, it must be aware that the upswing will not last forever. How and—even more important—when it identifies the emergence of the mature phase and the beginning of the downturn in its geographic region or product type will determine how well it is able to survive and, ideally, prosper in the downturn. There are four subsequent cycle strategy stages, to which companies should respond in a sequential manner.

Flashing Yellow—Hesitate and Reevaluate

In this second stage, companies should carefully assess the trigger events that they have identified. Depending on the type of company, certain strategies may be implemented to slow growth as a result of specific changes in economic activity or real estate conditions that trigger the company to deploy new strategic activities. For example, an initial, stage two strategic activity for a commercial real estate company could be to slow acquisitions and development activity by raising hurdle rates and to accelerate the sale of underperforming assets. In terms of personnel, the company may slow hiring and look for efficiencies in the organizational structure. There will, of course, be some differences between companies that "build and sell" and those that "build and hold." Owners of existing assets will need to determine whether they can weather an upcoming storm or whether they need to sell assets to improve liquidity, lower debt load to manageable levels, or create a war chest for strategic acquisitions during the next recovery phase. This could be a good time to sell for those who need to sell, while rental rate growth and occupancies are still holding.

Some buyers of commercial real estate may consider this stage the best time to take advantage of opportunities created by the departure of players that had underperforming assets and are seeking to redeploy capital. However, this could be a high-risk strategy if the eventual downturn turns out to be more severe than expected, particularly if the organization's interests are already heavily weighted in a specific geographic market. Development could provide higher returns than acquisition of existing assets, but companies must be sure that development returns are high enough to compensate for the increased short-term timing risk.

Similarly, a land development or homebuilding company will reassess its growth strategies at this stage. Market penetration is the sort of low-risk strategy that is best used in the face of an economy that is growing more slowly. Because total market sales are expected to decline in this situation, it is important to find ways to increase market share. While sales may be flat or falling, a company's market share could actually increase. One way to increase market share is through better market segmentation in the existing geographic market and the same product segment. For example, developers of master-planned communities may consider adding a retiree component (in either a separate neighborhood section or a spin-off or in a subcommunity) to existing projects. Retiree housing demand is a long-term trend, existing home sales are not expected to fall dramatically, and with the proper expertise, parcel sales to retirement housing developers could offset falling primary home sales. During this stage, companies should continue to monitor their indicators for further changes that will trigger the next stage.

Solid Yellow—Adjust

Determining when the third stage begins requires an assessment of the trigger events specific to an individual company or market. When this stage is reached, real estate firms should halt further acquisitions. It is critical to know when the time to buy has passed and to admit that a company is paying too much to achieve growth. If the timing is wrong, that "one last project" can drain the capital from an otherwise healthy company. Given slowing demand and new products in the pipeline, companies should anticipate lower occupancies or difficulty in achieving rental rate increases. Offering new services could be a route to expanding revenues from properties that are being held for the time being.

For some companies, this stage is the time to dispose of assets, even at lower values than could have been obtained just a few months earlier. This may be the time to consider expansion into other industry roles in order to reinvest capital acquired from those dispositions. Those roles could include servicing the assets just sold, especially if the buyer is an institutional or offshore organization. Sellers of assets need to determine the proper strategy: Which assets perform or contribute to company strategy and help maintain market presence or dominance, and which should be sold? At this point, the company needs to evaluate its entire portfolio with an eye toward reinvestment.

In this stage, real changes are made to the company structure, and there could be opportunities to redeploy some resources, including people and money. These changes also necessitate reducing general and administrative (G&A) expenses to an appropriate level for the company size. If downsizing is in the cards, the organization's morale could be hard hit. Companies need to consider ways to communicate changes of direction and facilitate employee buy-in to the potentially hard decisions that may be coming down the road.

If companies have not done so before this stage, they certainly will want to ensure that they have sufficient capital to take the organization through the downturn. Refinancing as appropriate with new equity capital is expensive but may be the only means of survival.

It will be a difficult task for land development companies to match their staff, finances, and land inventory to demand levels at this stage, because they are responding to a slowing economy but not a recession. Smaller land development companies that lack deep financial resources may have to consider downsizing if the economy slows further. The most successful land development companies may be those positioned to take advantage of the next upturn. Those that downsize too much may not be able to ramp up quickly enough to capitalize on new opportunities. Yet excess land wholly owned by the company that cannot immediately be put into production should be sold at this stage. Companies should continue monitoring their indicators to be prepared if and when it becomes necessary to move to the next stage.

Flashing Red—Rationalize

This fourth stage is much more severe, one that is entered into in the face of a serious recession or other adversity facing a company. At this stage, a company should begin serious rationalization of its activities or assets—beyond merely hesitating and making some adjustments. Organizations that reach this stage without having deployed intermediary cycle strategies will be ill prepared. Companies that do not position themselves to take advantage of such adverse conditions will instead become those that create opportunities for others.

At this stage, all strategic activities must be reevaluated. Activities that made sense in a growing economy and that still worked in a slowing economy may make little sense in a severe downturn. The company should now be focused on weathering the downturn. Hard decisions, such as closing regional offices, must be made. Some personnel reductions are likely in the preceding stages. At this point it is time to reduce personnel to the organization's core productive capacity and to further reduce G&A expenses to suit the company's smaller size. Functions that are not part of the company's core productive capacities probably are candidates for outsourcing at this stage. The hurdle rates required to justify development—which were raised at each preceding stage—should be raised again, further slowing development activity. Salaries for senior managers may need to be reduced. Companies should continue to monitor their indicators, to be prepared if and when it will be necessary to move to the final stage.

Solid Red—Survive

The fifith cycle stage is pure rationalization, which happens only when a company's survival is in doubt. At this stage the market has turned so severely that senior management must seriously evaluate the company's future as a going concern. The company should seek a merger or acquisition opportunity to recapitalize the company or to merge it into a healthier organization. Lacking those options, new development activities are abandoned and further cuts in G&A expenses are made to match operating costs to the size of the company. The company also sells off or leverages all assets, including the unleveraged stable assets that produce the greatest source of cash flow. Companies rarely emerge from this stage without radical changes. Most simply do not survive.

Other Types of Cycle Strategies

Real estate companies can use a variety of other types of cycle strategies to prepare for or react to a downturn in the industry as a whole or in their particular market or product type (see box at right).

OTHER CYCLE STRATEGIES

- Maintenance
- Geographic market downsizing
- Product or product segment downsizing
- Reduction in industry roles
- War chest

Maintenance Strategy

As its name suggests, the maintenance strategy maintains a company's competitive position in existing geographic markets, products, and product segments. The company retains its current market share and rises and falls with the market. An example is a rental apartment development and management firm that wants to maintain its 10 percent market share in a particular metropolitan area, even though the firm's overall starts may decline over a few years. This strategy fosters more realistic matching of staff, finances, and land inventory to existing demand and, by eliminating the need for radically gearing up or slowing down, allows for a less hectic organizational environment. Further, when a company pursues the maintenance strategy, it faces extremely low risk to its future survival.

Geographic Market Downsizing Strategy

The essence of this strategy—and the two related strategies following—is that a company scales back its activities in geographic areas and in projects and industry roles where and for which it sees limited current and future demand. Downsizing geographic markets reduces the markets served by a company to those that are most profitable. In a cyclical business such as real estate, a company's willingness to leave a recessionary metropolitan area may be crucial to its survival, particularly if the firm's activity in that region is capital risk–oriented. This strategy has two steps. A company first must determine whether a market in which it does business is getting into trouble. If it is, the company must reassess the market's long-term potential and decide whether this is a minor, cyclical shift—in which case it may choose to remain there but reduce its involvement temporarily—or whether this is a radical, long-term structural change. If the latter is the case, the company's best response might be to say, "We're out of here." Although the geographic market downsizing strategy results in decreased revenue volume, it can free up a firm's working capital. This strategy carries low risk, except when lingering problem projects are still being completed or worked out.

Product or Product Segment Downsizing Strategy

This strategy reduces the number of products that a company develops or manages to those that are most profitable. The strategy is particularly important to companies that are active in only one metropolitan area but that pursue many different product types. These companies generally have the flexibility to drop and add product lines nimbly as demand dictates.

Reduction in Industry Roles Strategy

In adopting this strategy, a company reduces or eliminates industry roles, particularly capital risk roles. Like the other cycle strategies, reduction of the company's capital risk roles or service businesses may free up working capital, but it also may lead to writedowns in value as well as extremely high shutdown costs.

One company that has used many—if not all—of the strategies described here is the Artery Group. In the mid-1980s, Artery was in the land development business and the apartment business and the homebuilding business; it had a large, diversified portfolio. Then came the credit crunch and the capital markets collapse. By the mid-1990s, Artery had rationalized its way out of several of its core businesses and scaled back on others. The company was out of the homebuilding business altogether and had a limited, symbolic presence in the land development business. It had lost most of its income-producing portfolio but was able to hold onto a portion of its apartment portfolio. Between 1995 and 2005, Artery diligently rebuilt its land development business. As opportunities appeared, it began to develop and acquire apartment, hotel, and office projects, but its core business remained land development. Having learned its lesson in the 1990s, by 2007 Artery had once again rationalized its portfolio, unloading most of its income-producing assets in a very attractive seller's environment.

The company now holds few, if any, apartment, office, or shopping center properties; what remains in its portfolio is its land development operation. Because of market realities in 2004–07, Artery was unable to find land to buy and thus is focused primarily on the orderly liquidation and sales of the portfolio of land development deals that were acquired and put into the pipeline before 2004. Yet the company continues to keep its finger on the pulse of the market and has not stripped itself of its core capabilities so that, when the market returns, it will not have to start over from scratch.

War Chest

As indicated above, an effective cycle strategy can involve going on the offensive and taking advantage of the misfortune of those who have not planned effectively for the downturn. This strategy involves maintaining access to a ready supply of capital, which can be accomplished through conservative balance sheet management or by accessing capital from partners or investors. This is the fundamental underlying strategy used by "opportunity funds."

The Final Word

A final reason for pursuing cycle or downsizing strategies is to sharpen a company's focus. Lack of focus plagues many real estate company strategies. Given their opportunistic nature, many industry players—particularly capital risk developers—are constantly looking for new projects. This opportunism, coupled with irrational exuberance, leads many to take a shotgun approach and simultaneously pursue many different avenues—possibly too many.

Focus is critical in any business endeavor. Although opportunistic research and development ventures should not be totally discouraged, they must not dominate a firm's activities. If more than 25 percent of a company's activity is opportunistic (that is, not in the company's strategic plan), the company is devoting insufficient resources to its primary pursuits and will not be able to meet its carefully considered strategic goals.

The best strategy for surviving a downturn is to avoid getting into trouble in the first place. Early planning and ongoing monitoring help provide management with the tools to avoid getting in trouble. Companies first need to develop a comprehensive strategy for all portions of the real estate cycle. Then, they need to be wise about when they shift their activities from one strategic initiation to the next, from growth strategies to cycle strategies. Last, they need to anticipate the downturn so they can be among the first to realize what is going on and do something about it before it is too late. As companies plan and implement their cycle strategies, they must be prepared to act decisively; history has shown how companies that hesitated too long ultimately failed in their mission.

CHAPTER 11

The Strategic Planning Process

The previous chapters outline the key elements of a well-rounded strategy plan for a real estate company. This final chapter deals with the strategy planning process itself and describes a successful approach that has survived the test of time as a proven method for conducting strategy planning for this unique industry.

The Plan as a Journey

Strategic planning determines where a company is going and how it plans to get there. A strategy plan is a road map that guides the company on this path. Development of a strategic plan usually takes the form of a focused process that runs over several months. Interestingly, most companies that have gone through a strategic planning process are not certain which was more valuable: the strategic plan or the planning process. As with travel, the trip itself may be as rewarding as reaching the destination.

The process explores the universe of options for the company; what emerges is an organic, dynamic plan for getting where the company is trying to go. No one would confidently state that the strategic plan adopted by a company's top managers precisely predicts the financial outcome that the company will achieve. But by focusing the company's efforts, preventing it from following every lead that comes its way, helping it understand the interrelationships within the strategy, and positioning it to adapt quickly to change, the strategic planning process places the company and its work in a well-understood context and charts the direction the company will pursue.

When?

Ideally, a real estate company should develop a strategy just before the current phase of the real estate cycle comes to an end: as the downturn seems to be yielding to the upturn, as the upturn ripens into the mature phase, before the mature phase falls into the downturn. Strategic planning should not be an annual exercise but rather one that should be undertaken at least every five years. Checkups should be done annually or biennially to confirm the validity of the strategy and to reaffirm the managers' commitment to the strategy. In fact, a company that finds itself revising its strategy every year or two probably has not done a very effective job of defining a true strategic direction; that company likely is mistaking business planning for strategic planning. The phases of the industry cycle and fundamental changes in the internal or external environment will dictate when it may be time to amend a company's strategy.

Strategy planning defines what a company does and, to some extent, where it does it and for whom. The question of how a company will execute its strategy is tactical—and though vitally important, not technically strategic. An ideal strategic plan should define strategies that will serve the company well in all phases of the economic and real estate market cycles. Often it is hard to have a clear line of sight to every phase of the cycle; however, the strategy should be flexible enough to guide a company through the current and likely coming phase, allowing for minor course corrections along the way. Only when it is clear that the phase of the cycle is beginning to change—or that the environment has changed fundamentally in a way that the strategic plan failed to account for—should the company adopt and deploy new strategies.

A company deciding to embark on a conscious formulation of strategy for the first time should not wait for the next phase of the cycle but should jump in and begin developing a strategy as soon as possible. A firm that remains rudderless for any length of time is not maximizing its potential and may, in fact, make potentially dangerous strategic mistakes.

If a new management team has just been put into place, it likely will want to engage in strategic planning immediately. It generally is best to wait until the new team has been in place long enough to understand the company issues and personalities before developing a new direction for the firm.

Finally, if a company finds itself unable to accomplish its goals, its strategic plan may have failed or may be inappropriate. The company should consider rethinking the strategy and engaging in a new strategic planning process.

Who?

Selecting those who will participate in the strategic planning process can be a sensitive matter. The first level of management (the "C-suite" managers, including the chief executive officer, chief operating officer, chief financial officer, and so forth) and the second level of management (managers of the major capital risk projects and operating businesses, other senior functional department heads, and the like) are almost always invited to participate. At times, however, it is prudent to also invite certain key "second chairs" and third-level management personnel to participate, for several reasons: their seniority; their access to particularly crucial information, such as knowledge of the market or an understanding of complex accounting issues; or the desire to increase buy-in and expose them to company leaders' decision-making process.

Three key factors should inform the composition of the strategy planning team:

- *Size.* Ten to 12 members is about the upper limit for a strategy planning team; the optimal group size is four to eight individuals. This has more to do with effective group dynamics than strategy planning; it is difficult for 12 or more people to have productive and sustained high-level conversations.
- *Strategic Thinkers.* Regardless of job title or experience, each individual invited to participate in the company's planning exercise should be capable of high-level strategic thinking. Even if a staff member is the most effective person in the organization at executing business plans, if that person is not able to contribute to thinking about and moving the company's strategy down the line, there is no point in including that person as part of the planning team.
- *Input.* It is advisable to "drill down" into the organization to seek input and advice on key elements of the company's strategy, without inviting everyone to participate in the entire planning process. Individual interviews, focus groups,

or workshops with various constituencies that inform the strategy typically yield valuable insights and help facilitate buy-in from those who were not involved in all aspects of the strategic planning process.

Buy-in to the company's strategic plan is critical to the success or failure of the strategy, but it is extremely difficult to conduct planning of this sort by consensus. Strategic planning should not be viewed as a democratic process; it needs to involve the company's most senior managers in a process that is informed and shaped by input from individuals or groups within the company.

It is crucial that the strategic plan be conceived by those who will implement it. An outside consultant could easily come up with a brilliant plan, but if the management team does not understand it or buy into it, it will not succeed. The world is full of examples of great strategic plans conceived by outsiders that did not work because of a lack of buy-in.

Finally, many consider it important that a company's strategic planning exercise be guided by a moderator who is an outsider but is made part of the strategy planning team. A chief executive, chief financial officer, or human resource manager who acts as moderator could bring hidden dynamics of the company into the discussion, which could bias the process and introduce a degree of distrust about the moderator's motives. As a result, some participants may be reluctant to voice their opinions and beliefs. An outside moderator can be far more objective than an insider in directing the conversation, steering the session to the strategy and action plan conclusions, and ensuring that the discussion is balanced—that all participants are heard and no one dominates the discussion or the strategy direction. If the moderator can offer insights about the economy and the real estate industry, then so much the better for all participants.

What? The Key Elements of the Process

The key steps in a strategic planning process, described below, apply as much to large companies with many business units or markets as to the small company whose senior managers wear more than one hat. Whatever the size and scope of the operations, the strategic planning process rests on several underlying assumptions:

- The strategic planning team is armed with sufficient background information and enjoys freedom of expression.

- Consensus decision making is feasible and achievable in the team.
- In the case of planning for a business unit or division, (a) the corporate strategy is well defined and spells out goals and objectives that can guide planning at the business unit or division level; (b) the business unit or division managers are qualified to determine business strategy within the limits of the ground rules set by corporate-level management and, therefore, will not be second guessed; and (c) the business unit's senior managers are sufficiently disciplined to implement the action plan.

The strategy planning process includes the seven steps described in the following sections (figure 11-1).

Figure 11-1: STRATEGY PLANNING PROCESS

1. Discovery
2. Situation Analysis
3. Preliminary Strategy Planning Session
4. Strategy Formulation
5. Final Strategy Planning Session
6. Documentation
7. Input and Approval
8. Business or Implementation Plan
9. Monitoring and Score Card

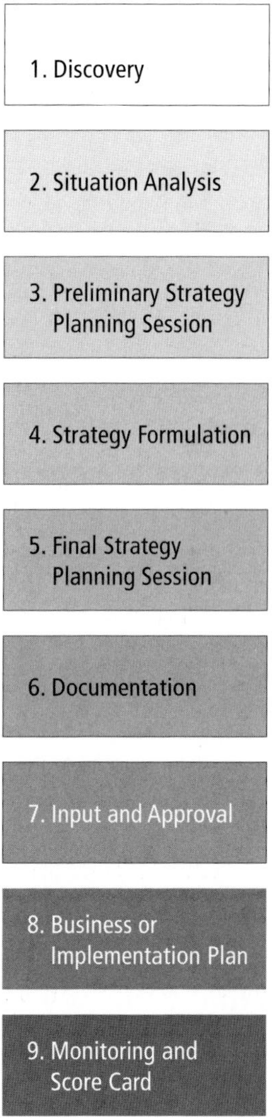

Discovery

The discovery step is focused on identifying the key issues that must be subjected to analysis and evaluation in the next step and in the subsequent planning sessions. The discovery step typically begins with a debriefing from the selected strategy team participants. This step also includes personal or group interviews with select resources, both inside and outside the company, which aim to identify the relevant issues to be addressed during the situation analysis and further strategy planning stages. It is often at this stage that an initial strategy hypothesis is identified and begins to take form.

Situation Analysis

During this step, the moderator and strategy team members—with support from internal and external resources, as necessary—analyze the issues raised during the discovery step and begin to formulate the preliminary strategy hypothesis. Through this process, the strategy team becomes familiar with and is able to analyze important aspects of the company, its historical and current performance, its management team, its organization, its core competencies, its capital structure, and so forth. The objective is to form an independent, objective view of the company, its structure, its strengths and weaknesses, and the constraints and opportunities (real and perceived) affecting it.

During the situation analysis, the company's implied strategy—the strategy that it is following, as evidenced by observing its actions, whether or not this is consistent with its written or stated strategy—becomes apparent. The strategy team drills down into opportunities, qualifying, quantifying, and defining them in terms of strategic possibilities (or initiatives) for future discussion and buy-in. During this effort, which leads into the preliminary strategy session, the team begins to identify key opportunities for technology, capital formation, and new geographic or product markets.

Every company faces unique challenges and opportunities, so the scope of the situation analysis also is different in each case. Typical analytical steps that many companies undertake in the situation analysis include the following.

SWOT Analysis and Core Competency Assessment. Before it draws a strategic road map for the business, the planning group must understand where the business is now, in terms of its competencies, in relation to competitors, and in relation to its industry and the economy as a whole. This element of the planning process involves identifying and analyzing the company's strengths, weaknesses, opportunities, and threats (SWOT). This effort includes an examination of the firm's core competencies—the skills and talents that afford it a competitive advantage in one or more areas—and its customer strategy. In addition to listing the current core competencies, the strategy team should prepare a list of target core competencies required to be successful in the future and analyze the degree to which the company already has these competencies. This effort will identify areas where the company (or specific divisions or other business units) needs to focus and where the biggest gaps exist.

Next, the team should assess the competition. What advantages and skills do the company's competitors possess? How do they measure up in terms of profitability and market penetration? What trends are emerging among competitors? When assessing competitors, it is important to think locally, regionally, nationally, and even internationally, as applicable.

In addition, the team should assess the particular segment or segments of the real estate industry and the underlying economy. An understanding of the current condition of the real estate industry and where it is going is critically important to successful strategic planning. Real estate is a very cyclical business and reacts strongly to even small changes in the underlying business cycle. It is important to recognize that a moderation of growth in the overall economy can create a recession in real estate, particularly if there is a rapid erosion in consumer confidence. Where real estate is in the business cycle certainly will affect strategic decisions. Consolidations and other changes in the structure of the industry also must be taken into account. In addition, the team should recognize that the form of the real estate industry may change over time, as may the sources and mechanisms of financing.

Internal Interviews. It may be difficult—or impractical—to invite everyone in the company to participate on the strategy planning team, yet various staff members may possess a tremendous amount of valuable information that could help inform the planning process. At a minimum, soliciting input or advice at various levels inside the organization will make people feel engaged in the process and facilitate buy-in to the final version of the strategy plan. Depending on the number of people from whom input is to be gathered and the positions or levels of these individuals, the strategy team can solicit their input using individual interviews, focus groups, town hall meetings, web surveys, and other techniques.

External Interviews. It is equally valuable to reach outside the company and conduct interviews with external resources, including key competitors, vendors, investors and lenders, with respect to the company's core competencies, brand and reputation, and performance in various product, price, and geographic market segments. For these interviews, an outside, third-party moderator can be particularly helpful, because friends and foes alike are more likely to provide candid input to a third party who guarantees the confidentiality of the feedback.

Assessment of Deployment and Peer-Group Industry Role. Often it can be very helpful to conduct an analysis of the company's current deployment—the lines of business, geographic diversity, product and market segments served, and so forth—focusing on assessing how well the company performs compared with its primary direct competitors in each major area of activity, geographic market, and product or market segments.

Forensic Financial Analysis and Cash Flow Quality. One of the most important things a company can do in conducting an effective strategy planning exercise is to understand where it is really making money (and where it is not), and how sensitive its revenue sources are to possible changing economic, real estate, or capital market conditions. The strategy team should analyze the firm's profitability, stratified by type of income (for example, income from stabilized assets, fee income, proceeds of land and home sales, proceeds from the sale of income-producing assets, and so forth) and by business unit, as well as for the entire company. In addition, the group should analyze where the company is making money by asset type, class, size, geography, and so forth. Finally, the group should examine where in the value creation chain the company makes money, in both absolute and relative terms.

From this effort, the group should attempt to isolate those activities that make the greatest contribution to the company's profitability, while also attempting to identify the areas where the company is relatively inefficient or may even be losing money. This analysis typically consists of an evaluation of cash flow, income, and return on investments and on invested assets.

Once the company is certain that it has isolated the profitability of discrete businesses and industry roles, the strategy team should analyze the company's financial sustainability under various sets of assumptions regarding the future of the underlying economy and real estate markets: (a) staying the course, with no significant changes in the economy or the company's performance; (b) a mild slowdown; and (c) a substantial downturn. The objective of this exercise is to understand the implications of each scenario for capital, reserves, and, ultimately, assets, given the current burn rate. The analysis should focus on three levels of assets: cash and other liquid securities, assets that are easy to sell, and assets that are hard to sell.

Portfolio Strategy Review. If a company does not regularly conduct an asset-by-asset or project-by-project analysis, the strategy team should do so. The goal of this analysis is to determine the position of each asset or project on what is commonly referred to as its "value–life-cycle curve," which includes an evaluation of the asset's current and likely future performance, deferred maintenance, capital requirements, debt, equity, or value position, tax or mortgage risk from sale, and so forth. At the end of this analysis, a preliminary asset strategy will be prepared for each asset. The portfolio strategy review will identify assets to be sold, held, restructured, refinanced, upgraded, and redeveloped. This process is important because it will lead to an analysis of capital available or required, as the case may be (equity and cash from refinancing, sale, and so forth), from or for the portfolio.

Benchmark Analysis. Again, where applicable and assuming the company does not do so on a regular basis, the strategy team should establish benchmarks against its relevant peer group for its various business lines and activities, in order to understand its relative position in the marketplace. For example, a company in the third-party property management business may choose to conduct a survey or prepare case studies to help it understand the property management fee levels, typical deal structures, profitability, and critical mass (that is, the number of units or square footage under management in a given market or submarket) necessary to achieve economies of scale.

Organization Case Studies. When a company is considering entering new lines of business, geographic markets, and so forth, it often can be instructive to identify best practices regarding organizational structure and deployment strategies. In these cases, the strategy team may decide to undertake case studies of selected relevant companies to determine how they are organized to address business line and geographical issues (such as asset management, investments, land acquisition, condominium versus apartment development, multiple locations, new geographic markets, and project versus functional orientation). These case studies also can be useful to benchmark and inform decisions about head count, overhead as a percentage of assets, and other key variables against which to measure or judge a company's overhead burden.

Market Opportunity Analysis. When companies are analyzing their current geographic deployment, market penetration, or possible expansion to new markets, it often is instructive to quantify the potential depth of the market for various products and services and determine what share of the activity in the market a company could expect to capture. If market expansion is a topic of discussion, macro-level indicators of real estate market supply and demand offer an objective way to narrow the focus. Armed with this information, a company then could estimate how much capital would be required to capture this market opportunity. The results of the situation analysis step are summarized in a briefing book that is disseminated to the strategy team members before the next step.

Preliminary Strategy Planning Session

The strategy team then convenes at a preliminary strategy planning session, which generally lasts about two days. This session should take place away from the company office so that the team can focus completely on the strategy process—which tends to be intensive—without distractions and interruptions. All participants should attend the entire session because it is crucial for them to hear everything that is discussed, so that everyone shares the same experience and the same information. Participants who lack key pieces of data may draw differing conclusions from the session, thus disrupting the strategic planning process. At the beginning of the retreat, the results of the situation analysis are presented and discussed, with a focus on the implications of the issues for the company's strategy.

Mission, Vision, and Values. Next in the session comes a discussion of the company's mission statement, vision statement, and core values or guiding principles. Strategy teams tend to take this discussion in one of two directions, either keeping the conversation at a very high conceptual level, delegating the details to a task group or individual off line, or doing fairly detailed word-smithing on the spot. In either case, it is important to allow enough time for the participants to discuss these critical elements of a strategy plan, but the debate should not be allowed to consume the entire planning session.

Goals and Objectives. Next the strategic planning group should identify the company's key goals and objectives. These typically are described in terms of quantifiable metrics that define both near- and long-term objectives. They can take the form of a statement about size and scale (for example, to develop 10 million square feet of space during the next five years); a relative market positioning statement (such as "to become one of the top five providers of property management services in a chosen market"); or financial and profitability measures (such as to maintain a weighted average return on equity of 20 percent). These goals and objectives must be informed by the objectives of the company stakeholders (owners, shareholders, partners, board members, and the like); the objectives can, in some cases, differ from the management team's personal or professional goals.

Strategy Pillars. The group then addresses the key strategy issues—the means to accomplish the company's goals and objectives—by providing a framework for establishing the actions or tactics that will be used on a day-to-day basis. This framework takes the form of the eight strategy pillars discussed in the previous chapters:

- *Industry Role Strategy:* What the company does;
- *Customer Strategy and Brand:* Who the company's customers and clients are and what their relationship is with the company;
- *Core Competency Strategy:* What the company does better, faster, or cheaper than its peers that affords it competitive advantages;
- *Growth and Geographic Deployment Strategy:* Where the company is active and how it grows;
- *Profitability Strategy:* How the company can improve efficiency and profitability;
- *Organizational Strategy:* How the company will maximize its effectiveness;
- *Capital Strategy:* How the company will finance its overall strategy; and
- *Cycle Strategy:* How the company will deal with the flip side of growth.

A preliminary strategy hypothesis is summarized at the conclusion of the preliminary strategy planning session. It is normally formulated as a set of strategic initiatives, their major implications on capital and organization, and the necessary rules of engagement (such as hurdle rates, capital allocation methodology, planning processes, and early warning systems). Often, this session will produce several action items, which are then assigned to various individuals for follow-up work. These action items tend to be organized in terms of the strategic initiatives, which are analyzed in the next step—strategy formulation—and which need to be completed in time for the final strategy session.

Strategy Formulation

The strategy team then completes the evaluation and analysis needed to validate the initial strategy hypothesis and formulate specific strategies for the initiatives under consideration. Typically, this is an iterative process, with teams (or task forces) gathering as needed to evaluate new information and to apply it toward the formulation of the strategy for each initiative. This process tends to last one to three months, depending on the depth and breadth of issues and topics. The strategy initiatives and action items then are rolled up into a cohesive strategy hypothesis during the final weeks of this process or at the beginning of the final strategy planning session.

Final Strategy Planning Session

The next step involves developing, finalizing, and adopting the overall strategy in a one- or two-day strategy planning session. Each strategy initiative is presented by the team members who were tasked with "homework" assignments and discussed both in the context of their merits and in terms of how they fit into the overall strategy. Economic, organizational, and capitalization aspects are considered as the overall strategy for the company is brought into its final form, seeking maximum synergy and scalability when appropriate.

Before the strategy hypothesis is validated and finalized, the strategy planning team should revisit and reconsider the initial mission, vision, and core value statements to ensure that they remain valid, given the assumptions and goals articulated in the strategy plan. If any of these statements seem invalid or unrealistic, they may need to be revised and aligned with the strategic plan. Similarly, the team should revisit and reconsider the initial list of core competencies and ensure that the company has the requisite core competencies to succeed (or has a plan to acquire or build these competencies). At the conclusion of this session, the strategy is finalized and adopted by the strategy team.

Documentation

The outcome of the strategic planning process is a strategy plan document, which should identify the company's goals and objectives and the strategies it will use to reach them. The intent of the plan should be to identify guiding principles of the organization that will pass the test of time and that reflect a point of view regarding future business decisions. At the conclusion of the strategic planning session, the team should prepare a final draft of the plan, then offer it for input and approval to a company's stakeholders, board, or other governing body.

Input and Approval

At the conclusion of the strategy planning effort—but before the plan is put into action and translated into a business plan—it is advisable to seek feedback from a wider audience within the company, in order to solicit buy-in. Once this feedback has been received and incorporated as appropriate, the strategy team presents and discusses the strategy plan developed during the preceding months and seeks input and further direction from the company's governing body, which may consist of the company's leadership group, owners, or an independent board of directors. With the governing body's input and approval, the strategy team's work is complete, and the management team then translates the strategy plan into a business plan and begins to implement it.

Business or Implementation Plan

Business plans differ from strategic plans. Strategy is set at or near the beginning of each phase of the real estate cycle; the expected life of a strategy plan typically is three to five years, since it changes only as the business context evolves. In contrast, the expected life of a business plan is much shorter. A business plan needs to be revisited at least annually to gauge whether it has been effective in moving the business closer to achieving its goals. Business planning establishes financial projections. Business plans build on the foundation laid by the strategic plan, laying out short-term tactical plans for strategy implementation. A year provides ample time to make changes in how the firm conducts itself while ensuring that financial projections are realistic. A year also is short enough so that the company can maintain enthusiasm for implementing a business plan.

Once all the strategy planning is completed and approved, managers must take the lead in translating the strategies and goals into a business plan. This is a critical element of the strategic planning process. Many strategies fall flat on implementation. The implementation plan should include monitoring progress to ensure momentum, as well as assigning responsibilities and setting measurable milestones for implementation that can be tied to key individuals' opportunities for compensation and promotion. Whereas strategic planning often is a top-down process, the determination of the tactics needed to achieve company goals should involve middle managers. They are ideally situated to recommend specific resources and methods to achieve goals. Middle managers thus must understand the goals of the strategic plan and be held accountable for their achievements, because much of the implementation will be their responsibility.

Follow-Up: Monitoring Process and Score Card

Regular assessments must be made of how well goals are achieved. Tactics should be reviewed annually; goals should be reviewed every two years or so. The responsibility for implementing the business unit strategy ultimately rests with the chief executive officer. It is the chief executive officer's job to make sure that the action plan is implemented in a timely manner. As part of that responsibility, the chief executive officer should conduct periodic reviews of the strategy to see if it needs modification, update the strategy session participants on the action plan's progress, and create new action plans as the items on the existing plan are completed. Because an action plan tends to entail assignments that require three to six months to complete, periodic update sessions should take place every three to six months. Of course, regular staff meetings also provide a forum for updating and reporting on the action plan.

Once in place, the strategy should carry the firm through the entire phase of the real estate cycle. Even though management will periodically discuss and modify the strategy, it will not need to set an entirely new corporate direction until the phase changes again—as it most definitely will.

CHAPTER 12

Case Studies

AvalonBay Communities, Inc.

A private company goes public, merges, and grows rapidly, remaining focused on its core strategy throughout.

The publicly traded AvalonBay Communities, Inc., has maintained its consistent strategic focus despite significant changes to its ownership format, geographic scope, and the size and scale of its operations. The company develops, acquires, repositions, and manages Class A rental apartment communities in high-barrier-to-entry markets (that is, high-cost, land-constrained markets with difficult entitlement processes) in the Northeast, Mid-Atlantic, Midwest, and Pacific Northwest regions, as well as in northern and southern California.

As of March 31, 2007, AvalonBay owned or held interest in 171 apartment communities containing 49,402 apartment homes in ten states and the District of Columbia, of which 16 communities were under construction and six were under reconstruction. AvalonBay's common stock trades on the New York Stock Exchange under the ticker symbol AVB. Its principal executive offices are located in Alexandria, Virginia; the company also maintains regional offices in or near Boston; Chicago; New York; Newport Beach, Los Angeles, and San Jose, California; Shelton, Connecticut; Melville, New York; Woodbridge, New Jersey; and Seattle.

The company went public as Avalon Properties, Inc., a roll-up of Trammell Crow Residential's Mid-Atlantic and Northeast divisions. Caught in the downturn of the early 1990s, the executives of Trammell Crow's Northeast division were frustrated by the mismatch between development opportunities and the availability of capital. Although they still saw plenty of prospects for the division to grow, financing was becoming increasingly difficult—if not impossible—and expensive to obtain on a deal-by-deal basis.

Chuck Berman, the Trammell Crow partner in charge of the Northeast division, saw an opportunity in this situation. REITs were just beginning to play a larger role in the real estate industry. Berman recognized that taking his division public could create a new business platform by accessing a new pool of relatively cheap, plentiful, and apparently endless capital—the public markets. Further, Berman reasoned that if this was a viable strategy for the Northeast division, it also would make sense for the Mid-Atlantic group—and that the combined divisions would offer greater scale, geographic diversity, and management experience, all of which would make them more attractive to Wall Street. Berman and Dick Michaux, a Trammell Crow national partner and the partner in charge of the company's Mid-Atlantic division, who also had oversight over the Northeast division, decided that taking the combined divisions public was a compelling opportunity.

In November 1993, Avalon Properties completed its initial public offering (IPO) at $20.50 per share on the New York Stock Exchange. At the time of the IPO, Avalon Properties had a portfolio of 22 communities containing 7,044 apartments in the Mid-Atlantic and Northeast and an initial value of about $500 million. Its strategic plan centered on maintaining the company's focus on developing and managing Class A rental apartments in markets with high barriers to entry. Michaux was chosen as the new firm's chairman and chief executive officer (CEO), with Berman as president.

Going public enabled Avalon to grow quickly through the mid-1990s. As a public company, Avalon was able to finance its operations without having to locate financial partners and negotiate joint venture and loan agreements, tasks that had distracted managers from their core development business and taken up a lot of their time. Bryce Blair, the company's current CEO—who was senior vice president of development in the company's Boston office at the time of the IPO—recalls that going public "also allowed us to take our management and our leadership to another level, in the sense of investing in the company's infrastructure—items like information technology, human resources and training, centralized design and purchasing. These things allowed us to take our game to a higher level, because we could now monitor our portfolio and make decisions in the aggregate, as opposed to having to say, 'Well, we can't do this with that deal because Prudential's our partner, or we can't do that with this deal because we have to check with another partner.' That prior structure had forced us to look at things on a deal-by-deal basis, which, somewhat counterintuitively, forced us to think more short term."

Going public thus gave Avalon's executives the freedom to think more about the company's long-term future. "What I most resent is when people say public companies think short term," comments Blair. "That isn't true in the real estate industry. Public real estate companies are thinking long term; many private companies are forced to think short term. Private companies are thinking, 'How do I finance this deal, when do I sell this deal?' They're not thinking, 'How do I create a world-class property management company? How do I invest $5 million in information systems that will allow me to be best in class?' When you look at innovations, whether in revenue management or branding, they've all come from public companies, not private ones. There's absolutely no doubt in my mind that we are a better, stronger, more long-term-thinking company today than we were as a private company."

Avalon's market strategy and development capabilities effectively distinguished the company from the many other rental apartment companies that had followed its lead and entered the public markets. By December 1997 there were 33 apartment REITs. Many of these REITs were much larger than Avalon, and companies such as Sam Zell's Equity Residential and Bill Sanders' Security Capital were gobbling up apartment assets, portfolios, and companies in their efforts to build national apartment portfolios in which size—and the resulting economies of scale—were at the core of their strategy. Berman and Michaux eventually realized that they too had the ability to create a national platform, but unlike Equity Residential and Security Capital (later Archstone), they would do so in markets with high barriers to entry, something that no other apartment company had done.

As the executive team members revisited their strategy, as they periodically do, they debated the importance of size and wondered if their current size ultimately would turn out to be a competitive disadvantage. The consensus of the leadership team was that size was important, but that it should not be the major thing that would define success for the company in the long run. The defining strategic vision for the company in the mid- to late 1990s was "bigger is better, but better is best." Although size was an issue in an era of rapid consolidation, it was much more important for the company to remain focused on its core strategy and to deliver superior returns to its shareholders than it was to grow simply for growth's sake. That did not mean that the company did not grow; it did. Avalon experienced rapid growth in its existing markets and expanded into the Midwest and then into the Pacific Northwest.

As the company entered the Pacific Northwest market, Avalon executives became aware of another firm that was in the process of penetrating that market. Bay Apartment Communities, Inc.—a California-based apartment REIT that was the successor apartment business of Greenbriar Homes. Bay had a strategy similar to Avalon's. At the time of its IPO in 1994, Bay had a portfolio of 14 communities containing 3,481 apartments in California. By 1997, it was expanding into Seattle, where it encountered Avalon.

The encounter in Seattle created "somewhat of a conflict of convenience," notes Blair. Berman and Michaux began meeting with Bay's CEO Gilbert M. (Mike) Meyer to discuss various business opportunities. As Avalon was endeavoring to create a national footprint in high-barrier-to-entry markets, Bay was dealing with its own rapid growth and attempting to determine what direction to take for the future. The leaders discovered that their firms were similar in many ways: both had entrepreneurial cultures, both were focused on development (although Bay had additional expertise in redeveloping and repositioning apartment communities), and both were a similar size. Avalon was finding that its ability to grow by developing communities in the West Coast markets was extremely difficult.

In June 1998, the two firms merged to form AvalonBay Communities. The "merger of equals"—each had a market capitalization of approximately $4 billion at the time—was unique in the world of REITs. No premium was paid on either side. While the merger gave the new company major benefits of scale and market penetration, it also created challenges. Integrating Avalon and Bay's corporate cultures and business practices became a painful and time-consuming endeavor. Because this was a merger of equals, neither side of the company could say "I'm the whale, you're the minnow, and you need to start doing things my way." Coming from thoughtful, analytical companies, both Avalon and Bay's executives wanted to explore each firm's best practices and combine the best of both. In hindsight, however, Michaux and Blair agree that in some cases they went too far, attempting to explore and analyze every aspect of the business while avoiding stepping on each other's toes. "If we had it to do over again," notes Blair, "we would not be as rigorous. We would say 'this is the way we're going to do this,' and only fight for the really important things. We were discussing far too many details."

How to integrate the two companies' leaders was another challenge. AvalonBay initially was led by an "office of the executive," consisting of Meyer as executive chairman of the board, Michaux as CEO, and Berman as president. This management-by-committee system created a void of clear, dispassionate, and decisive decision making; there were simply too many cooks in the kitchen. When Michaux announced his intention to retire in 2000, Blair was appointed the firm's president. Berman moved on to new challenges, and the office of the executive was replaced by a less complicated line of authority. Although some might say that AvalonBay is more Avalon than Bay—because the former company's key executives survived for many years beyond the merger while the latter's did not—the actual story is more complex.

One of the strengths that Bay sought from the merger was management expertise; the firm did not have as deep a management bench as Avalon, and Meyer and the rest of the Bay board recognized this as one of the key advantages in the merger. Yet the combined board of directors was made up of a majority of Bay's original board members; only one Avalon board member remains on the AvalonBay board, on which Meyer continues to serve. AvalonBay's present board thus is able to be truly independent and to make leadership decisions in the best interests of the company.

From its beginnings as Avalon Properties and Bay Communities through its current incarnation as AvalonBay Communities, the company has remained focused on strategic decisions while continually challenging and reevaluating those decisions, particularly with regard to where it operates, the type of product it builds and manages, who its customers are, and how it serves them. Its leaders have been disciplined in obtaining consensus about major strategic decisions among their key stakeholders and have analyzed opportunities carefully, rather than allowing themselves to get stuck in a rut or chasing the proverbial pot of gold.

One example of AvalonBay's deliberative nature occurred during the company's 2001 strategic planning update exercise, after which the company made a subtle but important modification to its mission statement. Before the planning exercise, AvalonBay's core purpose was "we build superior communities." The strategy team, with the support of the board, decided that the company needed to do a better job of customer service and responding to the needs and desires of its residents—that its business was less about bricks and sticks and more about its customers. As a result, the team modified the mission statement slightly to say that the company's core purpose is "enhancing the lives of our residents." It further reinforced this enhanced customer orientation in the firm's current strategic vision statement: "to more deeply penetrate our chosen markets through a broader range of products and services with an intense focus on our customer." AvalonBay thus began to focus more on customer knowledge—investing in surveys, focus groups, and demographic research to help it understand its existing and prospective residents—and on customer service. The firm's leaders became more disciplined about asking (and answering) the questions, "Where do we want to be, what do we want to build, who do we want to serve?" Demographic research convinced them that their future residents would be much more diverse in age, income, and ethnicity than their current residents and that that diversity would have a major impact on the products AvalonBay should be building and on the services it should provide. The company thus began expanding its product line from primarily suburban wood-frame garden apartments to mid-rise and high-rise structures, mixed-use development, and townhomes—with a greater variety of floor plans and unit sizes—in order to offer a broader mix of physical products to a broader range of prospective customers.

AvalonBay also remained disciplined with regard to its core strategy of markets with high barriers to entry, which had served it so well over time. This strategy did not go without debate and consideration over the years, in numerous strategy update and board member sessions. Rather than expanding into a broader range of geographic markets and relaxing its market strategy to diversify and achieve growth, the company chose to concentrate in fewer markets and to become more diverse—and dominant—in those markets. In the late 1990s and the first few years of the 21st century, AvalonBay sold assets in markets in which it had a limited presence, in order to concentrate its presence into 16 metropolitan statistical areas (down from 26). It began to focus more on scaling up in each of these 16 markets, rather than expand nationally or compromise its market strategy.

In addition to their focus on strategy, AvalonBay's leaders have paid a great deal of attention to how they execute their strategy, primarily by making sure that they have the right organization in place to make it happen. The company's stable management and clearly defined succession plans have enabled it to succeed in implementing its strategic objectives in different parts of the real estate cycle.

AvalonBay also has remained committed to the strategic planning process. Referring to the old adage, "If you don't know where you're going, any road will take you there." Blair comments, "We've done a pretty good job of knowing which mountains we're trying to climb, what destinations we want to get to, so we can pick the roads. We've been disciplined in our strategy but flexible in our execution." The company's strategic plans have not limited its opportunities; rather, they have enabled it to keep its focus on making the most of these opportunities over both the short and the long terms. In addition to consciously and deeply rethinking its strategy every five years, the firm does a less intensive annual strategy review—what Blair refers to as an annual tune-up—and a midlevel review every three years. Looking ahead, to 2010 and beyond, Blair contends that AvalonBay remains focused on the same issues it has faced since its early days: "Are we focused on the right customer? Are we delivering the right product? And do we have the right organization and capital structure in place to make it happen?"

The Bozzuto Group

A private regional development firm grows its capital risk business and retains ownership of assets while maintaining a strategic balance of operating risk activities.

The Bozzuto Group is a private, multidisciplinary real estate development and services company headquartered in the Washington, D.C., metropolitan area. Tom Bozzuto, CEO and founder, is a true believer in the value of diversification and strategic balance.

In 1988, Bozzuto, along with John Slidell, Rick Mostyn, and the late Bernard Lubcher, bought out the Mid-Atlantic region business of Oxford Development Corporation—where all four had worked, Bozzuto as regional partner—to form the Bozzuto Group. Their intent was to build and manage rental apartment communities.

Over the years, the group has maintained a highly successful strategic balance of relatively stable fee-income businesses and multiple capital risk businesses and product segments. Those segments included the acquisition and development of both luxury and affordable rental apartment communities, land development, and the construction and development of for-sale condominiums, townhomes, and single-family detached homes. In addition, it has a very successful third-party property management operation and a growing landscape business. This diversity of activities and segments has largely enabled it to weather real estate cycles and invest selectively in development opportunities.

Today, the Bozzuto Group consists of five interrelated companies: Bozzuto Homes, which builds single-family homes, townhomes, and condominiums; Bozzuto Development, which specializes in the development of high-end multifamily rental communities in both urban and suburban settings; Bozzuto Management, which is responsible for managing all Bozzuto-owned communities as well as properties for a variety of other third-party clients; Bozzuto Construction, which provides project planning and construction services for third-party owners as well as for projects being developed by the Bozzuto Group; and Bozzuto Acquisitions, which deals exclusively in the purchase and sale of multifamily residential properties, specializing in garden-style communities. In 2007, the company sold its landscaping business to the executives in charge of Bozzuto Landscaping, which had been providing landscaping design, enhancement, and commercial grounds maintenance services to a diverse client base. The group has a sterling reputation as an experienced "white hat" developer and manager. Although the company's original focus had been on the Washington, D.C., and Baltimore region, it is now expanding outside its home base into other parts of the Mid-Atlantic and Northeast.

Several years after forming the Bozzuto Group, the founding partners recognized that they had a valuable presence in the market and a recognizable and respected brand that was able to generate premium pricing and occupancy in the communities they built and managed. During the mid-1990s, however, they began to notice that some of their development industry peers seemed to be outperforming them and getting larger shares of deals or profits, without having to put their own capital at risk. The partners suspected that they were paying too much for capital, and they knew that they were taking on more risk than they wanted; the partners themselves were guaranteeing loans, not the company. They realized that they needed to focus on their capital strategy by broadening their joint venture partnership strategy, seeking less expensive "other people's money" and securing nonrecourse debt. Through a process of discovery, they realized that there were investors who were eager to partner with them and who were willing to take bigger risks, without significant coinvestments and without the Bozzuto partners having to sign personal guarantees. Such investors would enable the Bozzuto Group to be fairly compensated, in the form of sweat equity and participation in projects, for its excellent reputation and its track record for successful development.

This realization gave Bozzuto's leaders the confidence to become more aggressive and proactive in identifying capital sources that would be more generous and that would better recognize what they had to offer than did their existing sources of capital. They learned that they could leverage their track record and reputation into more advantageous positions in development deals using other people's money; since that time the company has stepped up its relationships with several large institutional equity partners.

Recently, the Bozzuto Group formed a joint venture with the New York State Teachers' Retirement System (NYSTRS) to develop a range of multifamily properties in high-growth areas of the Mid-Atlantic, with a specific focus on the Washington and Baltimore region as well as on Pennsylvania, Delaware, and New Jersey. The total equity investment in the venture was $100 million (including $95 million from NYSTRS and $5 million from Bozzuto), which, when leveraged, was expected to support the development of approximately $400 million in new real estate assets. The new venture's first project is the apartment portion of a town center project in Herndon, Virginia, which is expected to be completed in the fall of 2008. This is the second joint venture between Bozzuto and NYSTRS; the first produced two projects: a 243-unit luxury apartment building in downtown Wheaton, Maryland, and a three-building, 241-unit apartment project in Arlington, Virginia.

The company's founding partner and CEO, Tom Bozzuto, believes that perhaps the most important goal that came out of the Bozzuto Group's strategic planning exercise was the determination that the company should own more assets on its own and hold them, both for long-term wealth creation and to generate a steady stream of income that can be invested in additional opportunities for capital risk development. Although in some respects that decision contradicts the company's desire to take better advantage of the capital markets and use other people's money, it has enabled Bozzuto to develop projects in which the company maintains far more control over the real estate than it does in the projects it develops with its institutional partners. In pursuit of this ownership strategy, the company has developed half a dozen projects in partnership with landowners who share its goal of owning assets over the long term.

Another important element of the company's strategic planning process was examining a range of organizational issues, including employee retention and succession planning. For most of its history, the Bozzuto Group prided itself on paying decent salaries but offered its employees no bonuses whatsoever, no profit-sharing opportunities, and certainly no ownership in deals. This seemed to serve the company well for many years, and Bozzuto remains to this day an employer of choice for its excellent reputation and unique corporate culture. For loyal Bozzuto employees, working there was not just about the money; it was about being part of a special organization. By the 1990s, however, Bozzuto's compensation strategy seemed to be out of step with what was happening elsewhere in the real estate industry. The company was finding it increasingly difficult to recruit and retain key employees, and even feared losing a handful of key senior executives critical to the company's future to other companies that were willing to offer more rewarding compensation plans, including profit sharing and ownership. Facing this realization, the founding partners decided to change their compensation structure and to invite some of the most valuable senior executives into the inner circle, to share in the organization's ownership and profits.

The critical strategic issue was how to retain valuable employees with an eye toward succession: grooming the next generation of leaders while making it worthwhile for them to stay with the company. The firm expanded its leadership group by creating several new partner positions. Today, the company has seven partners. It also added a third tier of leaders, who are eligible to participate in cash profits from the company on an annual basis, and recently created another compensation step that enables some of those individuals to also have an ownership interest in the projects that the company develops and owns.

Despite all these changes, retention continues to be the firm's biggest challenge. Realizing that nothing the firm does will keep all its key employees from being lured away by potentially lucrative offers, the group prides itself on its retention rate, which is a testament to the organization's positive corporate culture. A significant percentage of Bozzuto's employees have been with the company for more than seven years, and it maintains contact with former employees so that they realize they will be welcomed back if they choose to return.

Succession planning is another important strategic issue for the company going forward. The organization now has an excellent second tier of partners that includes the sons of two of the founding partners. Tom Bozzuto's son Toby, as executive vice president of Bozzuto Development Company, now oversees day-today development activities for the company's apartment development operations. Duncan Slidell, son of founding partner Rick Slidell, also is involved in the business. Although the involvement of family members often can be a touchy subject in the context of strategic planning, Tom Bozzuto made a conscious decision to indicate publicly that he intends for Toby to take over his ownership stake in the business eventually and occupy the leadership of the firm one day. At the same time, Tom is quick to point out that he has no current plans to retire and, perhaps more important, is cognizant that Toby still has much to learn and needs to earn his stripes and the confidence of those in the company. Addressing these intentions openly in the context of the strategic planning process has been beneficial to the organization, because no one has to guess what the plan is for succession.

Growth and geographic deployment strategies also are important elements of Bozzuto's long-term strategic plan. In 2000, the first time the company engaged in formal strategic planning, its leaders agreed that they should stay focused on the Washington and Baltimore region, although they had already begun thinking about expanding into other markets. They therefore decided to lay out the parameters for growth beyond their home region but said, in effect, "not now, but soon." Three years later, while revisiting their strategic plan, they recognized that, having solidified their position in their home market, they were ready to begin expanding to other geographic areas.

Bozzuto's expansion strategy involves leveraging its investor relationships and entering new markets through its property-management fee business or in partnership with its principal investors. This strategy has enabled it to minimize its risks, learn the new market, and build a presence there, which then may lead to acquisition or development opportunities. For example, one of Bozzuto's principal capital sources, which had worked extensively with the company in Washington, requested that Bozzuto get involved with it on a development project in Philadelphia. Bozzuto agreed, even though the firm did not have a significant presence in that market. As they became familiar with the market as a result of this development project, Bozzuto's leaders became aware that there was not a lot of competition in it and thus decided to make a much more significant move into Philadelphia. The firm attempted to use this same strategy to enter the New England market, by developing a project with one of its capital partners and, in a low-risk manner, gaining a toehold in the market on which it could build. Unfortunately for Bozzuto, however, the partner, which controlled the decision, decided to sell the project after it was completed. Although Bozzuto made a nice profit on the deal, it lost its toehold in New England. One of its strategic objectives going forward is to devote resources to identifying new opportunities there.

Another issue that Bozzuto confronted during its initial strategic planning process was a company culture that was relatively risk averse, to the extent of being unduly timid in its business ventures. The founding partners continuously questioned and second-guessed each of their businesses, asking themselves, "Should we really be a third-party provider of property management services, a construction company, a landscaping company?" What came out of their discussions during the strategic planning process were the realizations first, that all these businesses are, in fact, viable operations and second, that their recent historical performance proved that strategic balance was a winning strategy, even though they had come about it somewhat unconsciously. The resulting strategic plan confirmed that diversity and a combination of service income and capital risk activities that leverage other people's money is a winning formula for the long term.

That is not to say that there was no debate about certain activities and business lines among the strategy team participants. For example, the company's leaders struggled with whether or not one of the group's operating risk businesses—its landscaping company—belonged in an organization focused on real estate development and property management. Early in the planning process, Bozzuto's leaders realized that they had to make a go/no-go decision about whether to retain or drop what was at the time a volatile and relatively small business compared with their other business lines, one that was largely dependent on business from the parent company. In a bad year, the landscaping business would struggle to break even; in a good year—one with a lot of snow—it would make only limited contributions to overall company profitability. Yet, at the same time, it required very little senior management attention because a competent, committed manager was running the operation. After some debate the strategy team decided, in the spirit of strategic balance, not to continue to let landscaping be a small adjunct to Bozzuto's core business but rather to grow the operation so that it could stand on its own and operate independently of Bozzuto's other businesses.

The partners challenged the management of the landscaping business to go out and create its own strategy for developing an independent customer base. Bozzuto Landscaping expanded its client base to include office and industrial parks, hospitals, schools, restaurants and other retail establishments, and military installations, in addition to Bozzuto's own apartment and condominium properties. One of the key factors in making the decision to keep landscaping as part of the mix initially was the fact that the division was headed by a real go-getter, a self-starter who ran the business without taking too much management attention away from Bozzuto's core homebuilding and apartment businesses. Had this not been the case, the organization probably would have jettisoned the business long ago. The company did ultimately decide to exit this business and sold the practice to its managers in 2007. While the distraction was limited, it still required attention from senior leaders in the firm, attention that was better spent on its core, high-value, capital risk activities.

The Bozzuto Group keeps its strategic plan fresh by revisiting and updating it every four or five years. During the intervening years, the three founding partners get away from the office several times a year to discuss strategic issues, and once a year the firm puts together a business plan through a bottom-up process that responds to issues covered in the strategic plan.

Looking back on his firm's activities since the early 1990s, Tom Bozzuto notes that the company has succeeded in maintaining its strategic balance between capital risk and operating risk businesses. Building income properties for its own account, being in the third-party service business, and being in the homebuilding business have served as hedges against downturns in any one business. As Bozzuto comments, "Our profits may not have been quite as great as they might have been had we been a one-legged horse, but on the other hand we're always making money someplace. Maybe we're not hitting grand slams, but we're certainly hitting singles and doubles pretty repeatedly."

The company faced some serious challenges during the middle years of the first decade of the 21st century. "The biggest problem we've had," notes Bozzuto, "was working our way out of a bad condominium conversion project." In hindsight, it is clear now that the leaders decided to jump into the condominium conversion business at absolutely the wrong time. The company did succeed in completing the project without a loss, but the process was difficult and painful and it could have been an expensive mistake.

Bozzuto also thinks that there were opportunities to improve the efficiency in the organization's homebuilding business. "We were making so much profit that we became undisciplined," he states. "We hired more people than we should have, and we got cavalier about cost increases because we knew we could pass them on to our customers through higher prices. I kept saying to my people, 'We've got the wind in our sails, but it's going to change and we need to take the steps to address that now,' but we never did." Like most companies in the height of the upturn phase of the cycle, the Bozzuto Group was focused on growth, not efficiency strategies.

As far as the firm's capital strategies are concerned, Bozzuto is proud of the organization's accomplishments in expanding and diversifying its capital base, including the addition of new institutional partners and partnerships with landowners that enable it to own projects long term. "The one thing I'm not as happy about," he comments, "is that we haven't built quite as much capital in the company as I would have hoped for four or five years ago." Although the company is not cash poor, it has done quite a bit of corporate borrowing to fuel its growth in recent years. "While our fee development activity grew, our ability to put the money to work for investment purposes grew faster," he says. "What we're trying to do for the future is to balance it better so we can retain more liquidity corporately. As we modify our focus [in 2007 and 2008], part of our goal is to strengthen our balance sheet."

Crosland, LLC

A local, family-owned homebuilder shifts its focus to land and vertical development, then makes a transition from family to professional management and evolves into a major regional player and partner in acquiring, developing, and managing a diverse range of real estate projects throughout the southeastern United States.

Crosland, LLC, is a diversified commercial and residential real estate company with a market value exceeding $1.5 billion. It traces its roots back to the 1930s, when John Crosland, Sr., began building houses in Charlotte, North Carolina. Under the leadership of Todd Mansfield, Crosland's current chairman and chief executive officer, the company has grown its product offerings and expanded its activities into mixed and multiuse development and large master-planned communities. It now builds and manages apartment communities, shopping centers, and office and industrial space. It also develops residential and commercial land and pursues a broad range of general contracting assignments. The company's geographic footprint has expanded from one office in Charlotte to five regional offices throughout the Southeast. One of the keys to the company's success has been its ability to leverage its financial resources and human capital and expertise while becoming a partner with other companies in executing projects.

Crosland upholds its founding family's commitment to affordable housing, community-oriented development, and responsible stewardship. The company enjoys long-term relationships with a variety of partners. It has offices in Charlotte and Raleigh, North Carolina; Orlando, and Tampa, Florida; and Nashville, Tennessee. It also does business in Durham, Greensboro, Winston-Salem, and Asheville, North Carolina; Greenville and Hilton Head, South Carolina; Jacksonville, Florida; and Richmond and Hot Springs, Virginia, as well as in New Hampshire and Kentucky.

Crosland has a long history of using strategy planning to guide its activities. While the company was conducting a strategic planning effort with Robert Charles Lesser and Company (RCLCO) in the 1980s, a forensic financial analysis of its operations made it clear that Crosland was not as effective a homebuilder as perceived. The company was reasonably profitable, when looking at a roll-up of its overall business. What the forensic financial analysis revealed is that the company was very good at identifying and purchasing land and at horizontal land development but not very efficient at the vertical building of homes. In fact, the company discovered that it made 110 percent of its profit each time it bought land and gave some of that profit back each time it built a home.

The appropriate new strategy was clear: get out of the homebuilding business and concentrate on horizontal land development, which is precisely what Crosland did. The company sold its homebuilding business and rights to the name for homebuilding to Centex Corporation and secured a long-term contract to provide Centex with finished lots. The analysis undertaken in Crosland's long-range strategic planning effort confirmed two points: (a) the company earned its profits from its land business, not from homebuilding, and (b) homebuilding margins were thin because of growing national competition in the market. Interestingly, when Crosland's noncompete provision with Centex burned off, it went back into the homebuilding business, though in a smaller and different way. It has since divested itself of this second foray into the homebuilding business under the Lillian Floyd Homes brand name, but principals in the company have maintained personal investments in certain homebuilding companies.

In the mid-1990s, the company's second-generation president, John Crosland, Jr., decided it was time to step back from actively running the firm. There was no obvious successor within the company, and John's children, who were accomplished in other fields, had no interest in actively managing the family real estate business. Crosland thus began a search to identify a professional manager from outside the Crosland fold who could assume the mantle of chief executive officer. Todd Mansfield, who had served with Security Capital Group in London, the Walt Disney Company, Hines, and Booz Allen Hamilton, took over in July 1999. Soon thereafter Mansfield initiated a new comprehensive strategic planning process to begin charting the future of Crosland, with input and approval from a newly established board of directors chaired by John Crosland, Jr.

As a key part of this strategic review, the strategy team examined the company business by business to determine the relative profitability of each one. The team had to assess the company's true capabilities and assets as well as what was required for each business to succeed, then decide how to build the company's core competencies to ensure the success of each business. Crosland's leaders decided to terminate particular businesses and activities in which they did not believe they could be successful on a sustained basis. A comprehensive analysis of human capital and capacity allowed the organization to position people where they would be best suited to contribute most effectively within the overall business strategy.

Throughout this process, the leadership team spent a great deal of time trying to determine where the best opportunities existed and where Crosland could maximize its risk-adjusted return on capital. One of the key decisions that emanated from this planning effort was that the company needed to become much more aggressive at recycling capital. Historically, Crosland tended to build and hold for the long term, which limited its ability to make new investments in new projects that might yield higher returns. Another key decision was to diversify geographically, both as a hedge against the vagaries of a single market and to provide a more expansive platform that would generate greater opportunities for growth.

Another critical aspect of Crosland's updated strategy involved addressing the company's organizational structure. While Crosland had been successful over the years in a fairly diverse set of businesses, it had evolved into a company consisting of a series of entrepreneurial divisions that generally operated as standalone silos. Mansfield observed that Crosland was not optimizing the potential synergies that he believed were possible among the various divisions; each worked relatively independently and autonomously, without sharing key market information, future pipeline leads, or best practices. Other than sharing the same name, they did not really function as one company. To address this issue, Crosland centralized certain support functions, eliminated inefficiencies and duplication, and institutionalized processes and a culture in which best practices and lessons learned (both successes and failures) were shared across the platform. As the company became more involved in mixed-use and multiuse development, it assembled teams with representatives from various business lines to collaborate on development projects. It also realigned compensation and incentives to foster collaboration and a focus on success at the company level, not just at the division or project levels.

The company's leaders also recognized that Crosland had deep expertise and a reputation for successful execution of projects that should afford it a preferred position in deals. Mansfield realized that the company did not always have to buy its way into lucrative development deals with money; it could gain access to deal flow by leveraging its expertise, knowledge, brand, contacts, and image, in addition to its balance sheet. Essentially, he saw that Crosland's capital was much more than financial; what was most important was the company's human and intellectual capital.

Beginning in the late 1990s and on into the first decade of the 21st century, Crosland has leveraged its core competency in the land development business and has taken that expertise to other locations and product segments. The company has expanded its geographic footprint by partnering on land development projects in markets where it did not otherwise have a presence. It has experienced rapid growth by leveraging Crosland's capital and know-how with local partners that have land or the ability to execute at a local level, and with capital partners with which Crosland can control parcels of land for future vertical development. Crosland has been strategically expanding from its Southeast stronghold since 2000, opening offices in Raleigh, Orlando, Tampa, and Nashville. The company has entered into a strategic partnership with Celebration Associates and others and is pursuing developments as far away as New Hampshire, where it is involved in the Bretton Woods/Mount Washington ski and golf resort. As Mansfield sees it, "Land control is critical to success in vertical development. Without the right land, no amount of expertise in design, entitlements, etc. will overcome the handicap from subpar land holdings."

Looking back on the company's strategic plan over the years, Mansfield cites the rapid pace of change in the past few years—compared with the long history of relative stability at the company—as one of the biggest challenges the organization has had to face. Facilitating the necessary interdivisional collaboration that is requisite for the highest degree of success also has been a challenge. Mansfield is quick to add that he would have liked the process to have moved more quickly but admits that this may not have been practical, given the company's financial success, ingrained corporate cultural habits, market conditions, and personnel constraints. Key successes that Crosland has achieved as a result of executing the strategy plan include its strong financial results, a very strong pipeline of future projects, and the successful integration of the company's various disciplines.

From an organizational and governance perspective, Mansfield believes that a well-thought-out strategic plan certainly helped the company make a smooth transition from a family-run operation to a professionally managed organization with an independent board of directors. "Creating an independent board that expected a growth strategy and attendant risk was a critical part of continuing and expanding upon the company's historical success," he comments, noting that the strategic plan has provided important benchmarks by which company leaders and the board can measure its success. Mansfield adds, "Strategic planning was really important for us as a process and a mechanism for introducing and managing change in the organization, and as way to introduce new ways of thinking about the business." Reflecting on the value of continuing to work with RCLCO, he says "We may have been able to come up with some of these conclusions independently of outside expertise, but I think RCLCO put a process in place and a rigor that forced engagement in collective thinking, which ultimately was probably the most important thing that had to change."

In April 2007, John Crosland, Jr., retired as chairman of Crosland and Mansfield added that role to his duties. "This company is on an excellent footing," said

Crosland at the time. "Under Todd's leadership, we've grown more significantly and successfully than even I thought possible. Retiring now affords me the opportunity to guide the organization through this next phase of my succession plan." Crosland continues to work from his office in the company headquarters and remains active as chairman emeritus. The family involvement in the firm will not end with John Crosland, Jr.; his son, John Crosland III, currently serves as vice chairman of the board of directors.

Looking back from the perspective of 2007 on the key strategic initiatives that were formulated in 2001, it is clear that the company has established an excellent track record. Throughout the course of the strategic plan horizon, among the most significant evolutionary changes that the company has brought are a heightened emphasis on leveraging third-party capital and an increased focus on larger-scale developments. Crosland has succeeded in diversifying its geographic and product focus; it is now active in seven states and has added second-home and resort businesses to its list of activities. The company has retained the Crosland culture and soul while making significant investments in both systems and people to achieve its plan. The company's net worth doubled in five years while shareholder dividends increased significantly, thus materially enhancing the platform for future growth. The firm has been able to leverage a strong foundation and legacy through its strategic planning effort.

Transwestern

A private company that began as a small Texas developer shifts its focus to services in the mid-1980s market collapse, engineers explosive growth to become a national diversified services company, parlays a national network of local market talent into a powerhouse investment company, and then circles back to its roots with a bold initiative in development. All in pursuit of "sustainability."

Founded in 1978, Transwestern Property Company developed 5 million square feet of space in more than 35 institutional-quality office and industrial projects in Houston, Dallas, Austin, and San Antonio until the real estate market collapsed in the mid-1980s. The company then transitioned into a third-party management, leasing, and investment sales business known as Transwestern Commercial Services LLC. Today, Transwestern is one of the largest privately held real estate operating companies in the United States, specializing in tenant advisory services, investment sales, agency leasing, property management, development, and research. Within the past several years, Transwestern has begun reestablishing its roots as a developer of office, industrial, retail, and health care properties. As of 2007, Transwestern employed 1,500 professionals in 22 offices and seven regions nationwide. The firm represents more than 250 institutional and private-equity clients and manages more than 750 projects totaling in excess of 130 million square feet. It has developed more than 50 projects totaling more than 10 million square feet since 2000.

By the mid-1980s, Transwestern Property Company had an experienced, talented team of people who were skilled at accessing the capital markets and developing, leasing, and managing its commercial real estate projects. The firm did no third-party work. Then the bottom fell out of the Texas real estate market. As Transwestern Chairman Robert Duncan recalls, "It was really ugly. It wasn't a downturn. In Texas, we had a collapse. Nothing looked good. The price of oil went from north of $20 to $6 a barrel in a matter of months. Interest rates soared and liquidity dried up. Businesses were laying off employees left and right. Tenants were bellying up. The banks were broke. The only thing of value was tax write-offs of losses and the Tax Act of '86 eliminated those. We went from buildings that were 95 percent leased at 20 to 30 percent above pro forma rents—cash cows—that turned into horror shows with big deficits within a period of 12 months." The company found itself extremely overleveraged and, suddenly, there was no need for what it did best—development. Transwestern was all dressed up with no place to go.

By 1986, it was clear that the company had to retool its operations and put an entirely new strategy in place if it was to survive. Unlike many of its competitors, Transwestern avoided bankruptcy. Nonetheless, it had to restructure all its debt and, as a result, lost nearly all its net worth. The company went into "survival mode" and, for the first time, looked to outside consultants—first Kenneth Leventhal and Company and later RCLCO—to help it take an objective look at itself and decide what to do next. Through this process, Duncan and his staff came to understand that what they were facing was not just a cyclical downturn, but a long-term change in the industry.

After examining the firm's experience and core competencies, its leaders recognized that, with so many projects in trouble throughout Texas and the Southwest,

Transwestern was well positioned to serve the growing market for third-party workout and asset management services. The company's new strategy therefore emphasized those services. Duncan notes that, at its inception, Transwestern Commercial Services already had an edge on much of the competition: "Because we were owners and operators, we thought and acted like owners and operators. We had an 'A Team' of people who were able to come in and provide a broader, more sophisticated delivery system for repositioning and problem solving than a typical third-party service company at the time. I believe Transwestern was a pace setter in establishing a new and higher standard in asset management."

The transition was not an easy one; people who saw themselves as developers had a hard time making the transition to becoming service providers. But as Duncan notes, "The real lesson we learned is that wherever you can bring the most value to the market is the right place to be." By the late 1980s, the company was riding a rocket ship of growth. Transwestern originally had developed and managed primarily office and industrial projects, with some retail. As a third-party service provider it began to diversify, taking on larger, mixed-use projects and large, diverse institutional portfolios. It also expanded geographically, from Texas into the greater Southwest, southern California, and eventually the Midwest and Southeast. The more work it took on, the more people it had to hire to manage, operate, and report on these operations. The firm's area under management expanded from roughly 5 million square feet in the late 1980s to more than 50 million square feet of commercial and industrial space by the early 1990s, making it one of the largest asset management companies in the nation.

In 1996, in response to a growing client base, Transwestern launched its "Millennium Plan," a blueprint for continuing its growth nationally and expanding its service lines. Although Transwestern had diversified geographically, it was not yet a national player. And although it had diversified its service base, it was still primarily in the property management, agency leasing, and brokerage businesses. As Duncan puts it, "We were a 'tenderfoot' in the tenant representation and corporate services businesses at the time, and there was still little development to do." For the first time, Transwestern began to consider acquiring or merging with other companies. It brought on a mergers and acquisitions team to search for companies, teams, and individuals who might be able to contribute to the firm's growth strategy. In 1998, the company continued its geographic and service expansion through a merger with Carey Winston Company, which established a Mid-Atlantic presence, and the acquisition of Delta Associates as the firm's research arm. Transwestern also continued to grow organically, attracting new clients with growing portfolios and offering them new and more sophisticated services. From 1998 through 2004, the company continued to expand significantly in its existing markets and moved into new markets, opening offices in Denver, Chicago, San Francisco, Atlanta, and Miami.

Meanwhile, in the early and mid-1990s Transwestern's leaders started to see new ownership opportunities. Many of its clients were new players who were buying troubled assets at very low prices—30, 40, 50 cents on the dollar—and then hiring Transwestern to market, lease, and manage them. No stranger to principal ownership, Transwestern began to selectively acquire undervalued assets in recovering markets. "It was exciting and frustrating at the same time," explained Duncan. "We now had super, highly capable people in markets all across the country who had the know-how to create big value. We kept uncovering attractive properties to buy, but we had severe limitations on execution in the asset acquisition business."

Investors wanted new and better vehicles for delivering attractive risk-adjusted returns in real estate. "They wanted investment partners with capital markets expertise, portfolio management skills, and local market connectivity," Duncan added. As the transaction markets heated up, sellers wanted to see the funds in place and they sought certainty of closing. And transaction time frames continued to shorten.

This convergence of change led Transwestern to form a new company—Transwestern Investment Company—which would create fund vehicles with ready cash to capitalize on emerging real estate opportunities in varying product types and in markets all across the country. "We knew we needed a full-fledged, fully integrated, sophisticated investment organization in order to compete on a national scale," explains Duncan. Thus, the formation of Transwestern Investment Company. Based in Chicago, home to cofounder and CEO Stephen Quazzo and other top principals and executives, Transwestern Investment Company raised more than $3 billion of equity in its first decade and acquired more than $10 billion worth of real estate. Modeled after private equity firms where its key players and contributors share in the profits, Transwestern Investment Company has been highly synergistic with its sister operating company.

Overall, Transwestern was doing a lot of things right. But ironically the very business that launched this burgeoning real estate enterprise—development—took a back seat to other activities. "Of course the markets would not support speculative development for years." said Duncan. "But even when the markets returned, it took us some time to rebuild the infrastructure necessary to capitalize on many of the underserved markets. We had been doing a good bit of development services work around the country, but we had to invest heavily in new talent and dedicated infrastructure to make principal development a core business again."

At the heart of Transwestern's unique business model is the integration of its re-emerging development capabilities into its successful service platform to become a truly evergreen company with optimal strategic balance. "We need to be in a position to move quickly to meet markets and we need to have the discipline and the flexibility to put on the brakes when we need to," says Duncan. "Each of our decentralized regions are implementing value-added strategies unique to the region. Our quality standards and operating philosophies are the same, but the local market focuses and strategies differ considerably."

Even the way the regions are building needed infrastructure differ dramatically. In cities like Houston, Dallas, Austin, and San Antonio, Transwestern has recruited local talent and redeployed veteran personnel. Yet in Washington, D.C., Transwestern merged with a prominent developer, DRI, to expand development capabilities throughout the Mid-Atlantic region. In southern California, Transwestern created a new development team by recruiting proven players with expertise in a wide array of product types.

Transwestern continues to have a collegial, unified, team-oriented culture, which Duncan sees as one of the keys to the company's success—and a continuing challenge to maintain. "The very biggest challenge all along, throughout the history of the company, has been forging rapid growth while retaining an energizing, collaborative, empowering culture where everybody is on the same sheet of music. It's something we work at constantly. Back when we were creating our Millennium Plan, we made it clear that we would not sacrifice culture for growth."

What is the biggest challenge the company faces today? Duncan says it is to figure out "how we continue to serve the ever-changing needs of our clients in a powerful and consistent fashion while remaining a fun, empowering company to work for and spend a career with, rather than a short bus ride. We want to be the right place to be for aspiring young talent who want to excel in this business, contribute to our success, and participate financially in that success." He believes that communication and planning are key to addressing this challenge and is proud of Transwestern's reputation as a company that puts significant time and effort into strategic planning and developing the careers of its people.